Guilt-Free Fat-Free COOKBOOK

Guilt-Free
Fat-Free COOKBOOK

Consultant Editor: Anne Sheasby

HERMES
HOUSE

This edition published by Hermes House in 2001

Published in the USA by Hermes House
Anness Publishing Inc.
27 West 20th Street
New York
NY 10011

Hermes House is an imprint of Anness Publishing Inc.

Publisher: Joanna Lorenz
Senior Editor: Linda Fraser
Designer: Sara Kidd
Photographers: Karl Adamson, Steve Baxter, Amanda Heywood, Michael Michaels, Don Last, Edward Allwright,
Thomas Odulate, James Duncan, Peter Reilly, Patrick McLeavey
Recipes: Carla Capalbo and Laura Washburn, Stephen Wheeler, Christine France,
Shirley Gill, Roz Denny, Annie Nichols, Linda Fraser, Catherine Atkinson, Maggie Pannell,
Kit Chan, Sue Maggs, Christine Ingram
Home Economists: Wendy Lee, Jane Stevenson, Elizabeth Wolf Cohen, Kit Chan assisted by Lucy McKelvie, Kathryn
Hawkins
Stylists: Blake Minton and Kirsty Rawlings, Fiona Tillett, Hilary Guy, Thomas Odulate, Madeleine Brehaut, Jo Harris

Front cover shows Spaghetti Alla Carbonara. For recipe see page 69
Previously published as *The Ultimate Fat-Free Cookbook*

1 3 5 7 9 10 8 6 4 2

NOTES
Standard spoon and cup measures are level.

Large eggs are used unless otherwise stated.

CONTENTS

INTRODUCTION

Cooking and eating good food is one of life's greatest pleasures – and there's nothing wrong with enjoying good food, except that for too long good often meant fatty. Butter, oil, cheese and other fatty foods were considered essential for good cooking. We know now that all this fat – along with too much sugar and salt – has a huge impact on health.

Most of us eat fats in one form or another every day. In fact, we need to consume a small amount of fat to maintain a healthy and balanced diet, but almost everyone can afford to, and should, reduce their fat intake, particularly of saturated fats. Weight for weight, dietary fats supply far more energy than all the other nutrients in our diet. If you eat a diet that is high in fats and don't exercise enough to use up

that energy, you will put on weight. By cutting down on fat, you can easily reduce your energy intake without affecting the other essential nutrients. And by choosing the right types of fat, using low fat and fat-free products whenever possible, and making small, simple changes to the way you cook and prepare food, you can reduce your overall fat intake quite dramatically and enjoy a much healthier diet without really noticing any difference.

As you will see, watching your fat intake doesn't have to mean dieting and deprivation. *The Ultimate Fat-Free Cookbook* opens with an informative introduction about basic healthy eating guidelines – you'll find out about the five main food groups, and how, by simply choosing a variety of foods from these groups every

day, you can ensure that you are eating all the nutrients you need. One way to enjoy your favorite foods without guilt is to substitute lower fat ingredients for higher fat ones. This book will introduce you to these lower fat ingredients and show you how to use them. There are hints and tips on how to cook with fat-free and low fat ingredients; techniques for using healthy, fat-free fruit purée in place of butter or margarine in all your favorite baking recipes; suggestions for which foods to cut down on and what to try instead; easy ways to reduce fat and saturated fat in your foods; new no fat and low fat cooking techniques and information on the best cookware for fat-free cooking; along with a delicious section on low fat and very low fat snacks.

There are over 200 easy-to-follow recipes for delicious dishes that your whole family can enjoy. Every recipe has been developed to fit into modern nutritional guidelines, and each one has at-a-glance nutritional information so you can instantly check the calories and fat content. The recipes are very low in fat – all contain less than five grams of fat per serving and many contain less than one. The selection of foods included will surprise you: there are barbecues and casseroles, pizza and pastas, tasty sautés and stews, vegetable dishes and vegetarian main courses, fish and seafood dishes galore and delicious breads, cookies and cakes. All without as much fat as traditional recipes, of course, but packed with flavor and vitality.

Fresh vegetables and beans (far left) and fresh fruit (left and above) make ideal choices for fat-free and low fat cooking.

HEALTHY EATING GUIDELINES

A healthy diet is one that provides the body with all the nutrients it needs to be able to grow and repair properly. By eating the right types, balance and proportions of foods, we are more likely to feel healthy, have plenty of energy and a higher resistance to illness that will help protect our body against developing diseases such as heart disease, cancers, bowel disorders and obesity.

By choosing a variety of foods every day, you will ensure that you are supplying your body with all the essential nutrients, including vitamins and minerals, it needs. To get the balance right, it is important to know just how much of each type of food you should be eating.

There are five main food groups (see right), and it is recommended that we eat plenty of fruit, vegetables (at least five portions a day, not including potatoes) and foods such as cereals, pasta, rice and potatoes; moderate amounts of meat, fish, poultry and dairy products; and only small amounts of foods containing fat or sugar. By choosing a good balance of foods from these groups every day, and choosing lower fat or lower sugar alternatives wherever possible, we will be supplying our bodies with all the nutrients they need for optimum health.

THE ROLE AND IMPORTANCE OF FAT IN OUR DIET

Fats shouldn't be cut out of our diets completely. We need a small amount of fat for general health and well-being – fat is a valuable source of energy, and also helps make food more palatable to eat. However, if you lower the fats, especially saturated fats, in your diet, you will feel healthier; it will help you lose weight and reduce the risk of developing some diseases.

THE FIVE MAIN FOOD GROUPS

● Fruit and vegetables

● Rice, potatoes, bread, pasta and other cereals

● Meat, poultry, fish and alternative proteins

● Milk and other dairy foods

● Foods which contain fat and foods which contain sugar

Aim to limit your daily intake of fats to no more than 30% of total calories. In real terms, this means that for an average intake of 2,000 calories per day, 30% of energy would come from 600 calories. Since each gram of fat provides 9 calories, your total daily intake should be no more than 66.6g fat. Your total intake of saturated fats should be no more than 10% of the total calories.

TYPES OF FAT

All fats in our foods are made up of building blocks of fatty acids and glycerol and their properties vary according to each combination.

There are two types of fat – saturated and unsaturated. The unsaturated group is divided into two types – polyunsaturated and monounsaturated fats.

There is always a combination of each of the three types of fat (saturated, polyunsaturated and monounsaturated fats) in any food, but the amount of each type varies greatly from one food to another.

Left: By choosing a variety of foods from the five main food groups, you will ensure that you are supplying your body with all the nutrients it needs.

SATURATED FATS

All fatty acids are made up of chains of carbon atoms. Each atom has one or more free "bonds" to link with other atoms, and by doing so the fatty acids transport nutrients to cells throughout the body. Without these free "bonds" the atom cannot form any links, that is to say it is completely "saturated." Because of this, the body finds it hard to process the fatty acid into energy, so it simply stores it as fat.

Saturated fats are the fats which you should reduce, as they can increase the level of cholesterol in the blood, which in turn can increase the risk of developing heart disease.

The main sources of saturated fats are animal products, such as meat, and fats, such as butter and lard that are solid at room temperature. However, there are also saturated fats of vegetable origin, notably coconut and palm oils, and some margarines and oils, which are processed by changing some of the unsaturated fatty acids to saturated ones – they are labeled "hydrogenated vegetable oil" and should be avoided.

POLYUNSATURATED FATS

There are two types of polyunsaturated fats, those of vegetable or plant origin (omega 6), such as sunflower oil, soft margarine and seeds, and those from oily fish (omega 3), such as herring, mackerel and sardines. Both fats are usually liquid at room temperature. Small quantities of polyunsaturated fats are essential for good health and are thought to help reduce the level of cholesterol in the blood.

MONOUNSATURATED FATS

Monounsaturated fats are also thought to have the beneficial effect of reducing the blood cholesterol level and this could explain why in some

Above: A selection of foods containing the three main types of fat found in foods.

Mediterranean countries there is such a low incidence of heart disease. Monounsaturated fats are found in foods such as olive oil, rapeseed oil, some nuts such as almonds and hazelnuts, oily fish and avocados.

CUTTING DOWN ON FATS AND SATURATED FATS IN THE DIET

About one quarter of the fat we eat comes from meat and meat products, one-fifth from dairy products and margarine and the rest from breads, biscuits, pastries and other foods. It is easy to cut down on obvious sources of fat in the diet, such as butter, oils, margarine, cream, whole milk and high fat cheese, but we also need to know

about – and watch out for – "hidden" fats. Hidden fats can be found in foods such as cakes, biscuits and nuts. Even lean, trimmed red meats may contain as much as 10% fat.

By being aware of foods which are high in fats and particularly saturated fats, and by making simple changes to your diet, you can reduce the total fat content of your diet quite considerably. Whenever possible, choose reduced fat or low fat alternatives to foods, such as milk, cheese and salad dressings, and fill up on very low fat foods, such as fruit and vegetables, and foods that are high in carbohydrate such as pasta, rice, bread and potatoes.

EASY WAYS TO CUT DOWN FAT AND SATURATED FAT IN THE DAILY DIET

There are lots of simple no-fuss ways of reducing the fat in your diet. Just follow the simple "eat less – try instead" suggestions below to discover how easy it is.

● EAT LESS – Butter, margarine and hard fats.

● TRY INSTEAD – Low fat spread, very low fat spread or polyunsaturated margarine. If you must use butter or solid margarine, make sure they are softened at room temperature and spread them very thinly. Better still, use fat-free spreads such as low fat soft cheese, reduced sugar jams or marmalades for sandwiches and toast.

● EAT LESS – Fatty meats and high fat products such as meat pâtés, hot pies and sausages.

● TRY INSTEAD – Low fat meats, such as chicken and turkey.

Use only the leanest cuts of such meats as lamb, beef and pork.

Always cut any visible fat and skin from meat before cooking.

Choose reduced fat sausages and meat products and eat fish more often.

Try using low fat protein products such as tofu in place of meat in savory recipes.

Make gravies using vegetable water or fat-free stock rather than using meat juices.

● EAT LESS – Full fat dairy products such as whole milk, cream, butter, hard margarine, sour cream, whole milk yogurts and hard cheese.

● TRY INSTEAD – Low fat or skim milk and milk products, low fat yogurts, low fat ricotta cheese and low fat soft cheeses, reduced fat hard cheeses such as Cheddar, and reduced fat creams and sour cream.

● EAT LESS – Solid cooking fats, such as lard or solid margarine.

● TRY INSTEAD – Polyunsaturated or monounsaturated oils, such as olive, sunflower or corn for cooking.

● EAT LESS – Rich salad dressings with full-fat mayonnaise, Thousand Island dressing or French dressing.

● TRY INSTEAD – Reduced fat or fat-free mayonnaise or dressings. Make salad dressings at home with low fat yogurt or ricotta cheese.

● EAT LESS – Fried foods.

● TRY INSTEAD – Fat-free cooking methods such as broiling, microwaving, steaming or baking whenever possible.

Try cooking in a nonstick wok with only a very small amount of oil.

Always roast or broil meat or poultry on a rack.

● EAT LESS – Deep-fried French fries and sautéed potatoes.

● TRY INSTEAD – Fat-free starchy foods such as pasta, couscous and rice. Choose baked or boiled potatoes.

● EAT LESS – Added fat in cooking.

● TRY INSTEAD – To cook with little or no fat. Use heavy or good quality nonstick pans, so that the food doesn't stick.

Try using a small amount of spray oil in cooking to control exactly how much fat you are using.

Use fat-free or low fat ingredients for cooking, such as fruit juice, low fat or fat-free stock, wine or even beer.

● EAT LESS – High fat snacks such as crisps, tortilla chips, fried snacks and pastries, chocolate cakes, muffins, doughnuts, sweet pastries and cookies – especially chocolate ones!

● TRY INSTEAD – Low fat and fat-free fresh or dried fruits, breadsticks or vegetable sticks.

Make your own home-baked low fat cakes and bakes.

If you do buy ready-made cakes and cookies, always choose low fat and reduced fat versions.

FAT-FREE COOKING METHODS

It's very easy to cook without fat – whenever possible, broil, bake, microwave or steam foods without the addition of fat, or try stir-frying without fat – use a little low fat or fat-free stock, wine or fruit juice instead.

● Working with heavy or good quality cookware, you'll find that the amount of fat needed for cooking foods can be kept to an absolute minimum. When making stews or meat sauces such as bolognese, dry-fry the meat to brown it and then drain off all the excess fat before adding the other ingredients. If you do need a little fat for cooking, choose an oil which is high in unsaturates such as corn, sunflower or olive oil and always use as little as possible.

● When baking low fat cakes and bakes, use good quality bakeware which doesn't need greasing before use, or use nonstick parchment paper and only lightly grease before lining.

● Look out for nonstick coated fabric sheet. This re-usable nonstick material is amazingly versatile, it can be cut to size and used to line cake pans, baking sheets or frying pans. Heat resistant up to 550°F and microwave safe, it will last for up to 5 years.

● When baking foods such as chicken or fish, rather than adding a pat of butter to the food, try baking the food in a loosely sealed package of foil or greaseproof paper and adding some wine or fruit juice and herbs or spices to the food before sealing the package.

● When broiling foods, the addition of fat is often unnecessary. If the food shows signs of drying, lightly brush with a small amount of unsaturated oil such as sunflower or corn oil.

Above: Invest in a few of these useful items of cookware for easy fat-free cooking: nonstick cookware and accurate measuring equipment are essential.

● Microwaved foods rarely need the addition of fat, so add herbs or spices for extra flavor and color.

● Steaming or boiling are easy, fat-free ways of cooking many foods, especially vegetables, fish and chicken.

● Try poaching foods, such as chicken, fish and fruit, in stock or syrup – it is another easy, fat-free cooking method.

● Try braising vegetables in the oven in low fat or fat-free stock, wine or simply water with the addition of some herbs.

● Sauté vegetables in low fat or fat-free stock, wine or fruit juice instead of fat or oil.

● Cook vegetables in a covered saucepan over low heat with a little water so they cook in their own juices.

● Marinate food such as meat or poultry in mixtures of alcohol, herbs or spices, and vinegar or fruit juice. This will help to tenderize the meat and add flavor and color and, in addition, the marinade can be used to baste the food while it is cooking.

● When serving vegetables such as boiled potatoes, carrots or peas, resist the temptation to add a pat of butter or margarine. Instead, sprinkle with chopped fresh herbs or ground spices.

COOKING WITH LOW FAT OR NON-FAT INGREDIENTS

Nowadays many foods are available in full fat and reduced fat or very low fat forms. In every supermarket you'll find a huge array of low fat dairy products, such as milk, cream, yogurt, hard and soft cheeses and ricotta cheese; reduced fat sweet or chocolate cookies; reduced fat or fat-free salad dressings and mayonnaise; reduced fat chips and snacks; low fat, half-fat or very low fat spreads; as well as such reduced fat ready-made food products as desserts.

Other foods, such as fresh fruit and vegetables, pasta, rice, potatoes and bread, naturally contain very little fat. Some foods, such as soy sauce, wine, cider, sherry, sugar, honey, syrup and jam, contain no fat at all. By combining these and other low fat foods you can create delicious dishes which contain very little fat.

Some low fat or reduced fat ingredients and products work better than others in cooking, but often a simple substitution of one for another will work. The addition of low fat or non-fat ingredients, such as herbs and spices, also add plenty of extra flavor and color to recipes.

LOW FAT SPREADS IN COOKING

There is a huge variety of low fat, reduced fat and half-fat spreads available in our supermarkets, along with some spreads that are very low in fat. Some are suitable for cooking, while others are suitable only for spreading.

Generally speaking, the very low fat spreads with a fat content of around 20% or less have a high water content and so are unsuitable for cooking and are suitable only for spreading.

Low fat or half-fat spreads with a fat content of around 40% are suitable for spreading and can be used for some cooking methods. They are suitable for recipes such as all-in-one cake and biscuit recipes, all-in-one sauce recipes, sautéing vegetables over low heat, choux pastry and some cake frostings.

When using these low fat spreads for cooking, the fat may behave slightly differently to full fat products such as butter or margarine.

With some recipes, the cooked result may be slightly different, but will still be very acceptable. Other recipes will be just as tasty and successful. For example, choux pastry made using half- or low fat spread is often slightly crisper and lighter in texture than traditional choux pastry, and a cheesecake cookie crust made with melted half- or low fat spread combined with crushed cookie crumbs, may be slightly softer in texture and less crispy than a cookie crust made using melted butter.

When heating half- or low fat spreads, never cook them over high heat. Always use a heavy pan over low heat to avoid the product burning, spitting or spoiling, and stir all the time. With all-in-one sauces, the mixture should be whisked continuously over low heat.

Half-fat or low fat spreads are not suitable for shallow or deep-fat frying, pastry making, rich fruit cakes, some cookies, shortcake, clarified butter and preserves such as lemon curd.

Remember that the storage times for recipes made using half- or low fat spreads may be reduced slightly, because of the lower fat content.

Almost all dairy products now come in low fat or reduced fat versions.

Another way to reduce the fat content of recipes, particularly cake recipes is to use a fruit purée in place of all or some of the fat in a recipe.

Many cake recipes work well using this method, but others may not be so successful. Pastry does not work well. Breads work very well, perhaps because the amount of fat is usually relatively small, as do some cookies and bars, such as brownies and flapjacks.

To make the dried fruit purée to use in recipes, chop 4 ounces ready-to-eat dried fruit and place in a blender or food processor with 5 tablespoons water and blend to a roughly smooth purée. Then, simply substitute the same weight of this dried fruit purée for all or just some of the amount of fat in the recipe. The purée will keep in the fridge for up to three days.

You can use prunes, dried apricots, dried peaches, or dried apples, or substitute mashed fresh fruit, such as ripe bananas or lightly cooked apples, without the added water.

Above: A selection of cooking oils and low fat spreads. Always check the packaging of low fat spreads – for cooking, they must have a fat content of about 40%.

LOW FAT AND VERY LOW FAT SNACKS

Instead of reaching for some chips, a high fat cookie or a chocolate bar when hunger strikes, choose one of these tasty low fat snacks to fill that hungry hole.

● A piece of fresh fruit or vegetable such as an apple, banana or carrot – keep chunks or sticks wrapped in a plastic bag in the fridge.

● Fresh fruit or vegetable chunks – skewer them on to toothpicks or short bamboo skewers to make them into mini kebabs.

● A handful of dried fruit such as raisins, apricots or sultanas. These also make a perfect addition to children's lunch boxes or to school break snacks.

● A portion of canned fruit in natural fruit juice – serve with a spoonful or two of fat-free yogurt.

● One or two crisp rice cakes – delicious on their own, or topped with honey, or reduced fat cheese.

● Crackers, such as water biscuits or crisp breads, spread with reduced sugar jam or marmalade.

● A bowl of whole-wheat breakfast cereal or no-added-sugar granola served with a little skimmed milk.

● Very low fat plain or fruit yogurt or ricotta cheese.

● A toasted teacake spread with reduced sugar jam or marmalade.

● Toasted pancake spread with fruit purée.

THE FAT AND CALORIE CONTENTS OF FOOD

The following figures show the weight of fat (g) and the energy content per 100g/4oz of each food.

VEGETABLES

	FAT (g)	ENERGY		FAT (g)	ENERGY
Broccoli	0.9	33 Kcals/138 kJ	Peas	1.5	83 Kcals/344 kJ
Cabbage	0.4	26 Kcals/109 kJ	Potatoes	0.2	75 Kcals/318 kJ
Carrots	0.3	35 Kcals/146 kJ	Fries, homemade	6.7	189 Kcals/796 kJ
Cauliflower	0.9	34 Kcals/142 kJ	Fries, retail	12.4	239 Kcals/1001 kJ
Cucumber	0.1	10 Kcals/40 kJ	Oven-chips, frozen, baked	4.2	162 Kcals/687 kJ
Mushrooms	0.5	13 Kcals/55 kJ	Tomatoes	0.3	17 Kcals/73 kJ
Onions	0.2	36 Kcals/151 kJ	Zucchini	0.4	18 Kcals/74 kJ

BEANS AND PULSES

	FAT (g)	ENERGY		FAT (g)	ENERGY
Black-eyed peas, cooked	1.8	116 Kcals/494 kJ	Lima beans, canned	0.5	77 Kcals/327 kJ
Chickpeas, canned	2.9	115 Kcals/487 kJ	Red kidney beans, canned	0.6	100 Kcals/424 kJ
Hummus	12.6	187 Kcals/781 kJ	Red lentils, cooked	0.4	100 Kcals/424 kJ

FISH AND SEAFOOD

	FAT (g)	ENERGY		FAT (g)	ENERGY
Cod fillets, fresh	0.7	80 Kcals/337 kJ	Shrimp	0.9	99 Kcals/418 kJ
Crab, canned	0.5	77 Kcals/326 kJ	Trout, grilled	5.4	135 Kcals/565 kJ
Haddock, fresh	0.6	81 Kcals/345 kJ	Tuna, canned in water	0.6	99 Kcals/422 kJ
Lemon sole, fresh	1.5	83 Kcals/351 kJ	Tuna, canned in oil	9.0	189 Kcals/794 kJ

MEAT PRODUCTS

	FAT (g)	ENERGY		FAT (g)	ENERGY
Bacon strip	39.5	414 Kcals/1710 kJ	Chicken fillet, raw	1.1	106 Kcals/449 kJ
Turkey bacon strip	1.0	99 Kcals/414 kJ	Chicken, roasted	12.5	218 Kcals/910 kJ
Beef, ground, raw	16.2	225 Kcals/934 kJ	Duck, meat only, raw	6.5	137 Kcals/575 kJ
Beef, ground, extra lean, raw	9.6	174 Kcals/728 kJ	Duck, roasted, meat,		
Rump steak, lean and marbled	10.1	174 Kcals/726 kJ	fat and skin	38.1	423 Kcals/1750 kJ
Rump steak, lean only	4.1	125 Kcals/526 kJ	Turkey, meat only, raw	1.6	105 Kcals/443 kJ
Lamb chops, loin, lean and fat	23.0	277 Kcals/1150 kJ	Liver, lamb, raw	6.2	137 Kcals/575 kJ
Lamb, average, lean, raw	8.3	156 Kcals/651 kJ	Salami	45.2	491 Kcals/2031 kJ
Pork chops, loin, lean and fat	21.7	270 Kcals/1119 kJ	Sausage roll, flaky pastry	36.4	477 Kcals/1985 kJ
Pork, average, lean, raw	4.0	123 Kcals/519 kJ			

DAIRY, FATS AND OILS

	FAT (g)	ENERGY		FAT (g)	ENERGY
Cream, heavy	48.0	449 Kcals/1849 kJ	Greek yogurt	9.1	115 Kcals/477 kJ
Cream, light	19.1	198 Kcals/817 kJ	Reduced fat Greek yogurt	5.0	80 Kcals/335 kJ
Cream, whipping	39.3	373 Kcals/1539 kJ	Butter	81.7	737 Kcals/3031 kJ
Crème fraîche	40.0	379 Kcals/156 kJ	Margarine	81.6	739 Kcals/3039 kJ
Reduced fat crème fraîche	15.0	165 Kcals/683 kJ	Low fat spread	40.5	390 Kcals/1605 kJ
Reduced fat heavy cream	24.0	243 Kcals/1002 kJ	Very low fat spread	25	273 Kcals/1128 kJ
Milk, skim	0.1	33 Kcals/130 kJ	Shortening	99.0	891 Kcals/3663 kJ
Milk, whole	3.9	66 Kcals/275 kJ	Corn oil	99.9	899 Kcals/3696 kJ
Brie	26.9	319 Kcals/1323 kJ	Olive oil	99.9	899 Kcals/3696 kJ
Cheddar cheese	34.4	412 Kcals/1708 kJ	Safflower oil	99.9	899 Kcals/3696 kJ
Cheddar-type, reduced fat	15.0	261 Kcals/1091 kJ	Eggs	10.8	147 Kcals/612 kJ
Cream cheese	47.4	439 Kcals/1807 kJ	Egg yolk	30.5	339 Kcals/1402 kJ
Skimmed milk soft cheese	Trace	74 Kcals/313 kJ	Egg white	Trace	36 Kcals/153 kJ
Edam cheese	25.4	333 Kcals/1382 kJ	Fat-free dressing	1.2	67 Kcals/282 kJ
Feta cheese	20.2	250 Kcals/1037 kJ	French dressing	49.4	462 Kcals/1902 kJ
Parmesan cheese	32.7	452 Kcals/1880 kJ	Mayonnaise	75.6	691 Kcals2843 kJ
Low fat yogurt, plain	0.8	56 Kcals/236 kJ	Mayonnaise, reduced calorie	28.1	288 Kcals/1188 kJ

CEREALS, BAKING AND PRESERVES

	FAT (g)	ENERGY		FAT (g)	ENERGY
Brown rice, uncooked	2.8	357 Kcals/1518 kJ	Flapjack	26.6	484 Kcals/2028 kJ
White rice, uncooked	3.6	383 Kcals/1630 kJ	Shortcake	26.1	498 Kcals/2087 kJ
Pasta, white, uncooked	1.8	342 Kcals/1456 kJ	Spongecake	16.9	393 Kcals/1652 kJ
Pasta, whole-wheat, uncooked	2.5	324 Kcal/1379 kJ	Fatless spongecake	6.1	294 Kcals/1245 kJ
Brown bread	2.0	218 Kcals/927 kJ	Doughnut, jelly	14.5	336 Kcals/1414 kJ
White bread	1.9	235 Kcals/1002 kJ	Sugar, white	0 3	94 Kcals/1680 kJ
Whole-wheat bread	2.5	215 Kcals914 kJ	Chocolate, sweet	30.7	520 Kcals/2177 kJ
Cornflakes	0.7	360 Kcals/1535 kJ	Chocolate, semisweet	28	510 Kcals/2157 kJ
Raisin bran	1.6	303 Kcals/1289 kJ	Honey	0	288 Kcals/1229 kJ
Swiss-style granola	5.9	363 Kcals/1540 kJ	Lemon curd	5.0	283 Kcals/1198 kJ
Croissant	20.3	360 Kcals/1505 kJ	Fruit jam	0 26	268 Kcals/1114 kJ

FRUIT AND NUTS

	FAT (g)	ENERGY		FAT (g)	ENERGY
Apples	0.1	47 Kcals/199 kJ	Pears	0.1	40 Kcals/169 kJ
Avocados	19.5	190 Kcals/784 kJ	Almonds	55.8	612 Kcals/2534 kJ
Bananas	0.3	95 Kcals/403 kJ	Brazil nuts	68.2	682 Kcals/2813 kJ
Dried mixed fruit	0.4	268 Kcals/1114 kJ	Hazelnuts	63.5	650 Kcals/2685 kJ
Grapefruit	0.1	30 Kcals/126 kJ	Pine nuts	68.6	688 Kcals/2840 kJ
Oranges	0.1	37 Kcals/158 kJ	Walnuts	68.5	688 Kcals/2837kJ
Peaches	0.1	33 Kcals/142 kJ	Peanut butter, smooth	53.7	623 Kcals/2581 kJ

SOUPS

Homemade soups are ideal served as a first course, a snack or a light lunch. They are filling, nutritious and low in fat and are delicious served with a chunk of fresh crusty bread. The wide variety of fresh vegetables available nowadays allows the freshest ingredients to be used to create tempting and delicious homemade soups. We include a tasty selection, including vegetable soups, chowders and bean and pasta soups. Choose from temptations such as Italian Vegetable Soup, Spicy Tomato and Lentil Soup, and Creamy Cod Chowder.

ITALIAN VEGETABLE SOUP

The success of this clear soup depends on the quality of the stock, so for the best results be sure you use homemade vegetable stock rather than bouillon cubes.

INGREDIENTS

Serves 4
1 small carrot
1 baby leek
1 celery stalk
2oz green cabbage
3¾ cups vegetable stock
1 bay leaf
1 cup cooked cannellini or
  navy beans
⅕ cup soup pasta, such as tiny shells,
  bows, stars or elbows
salt and black pepper
chopped fresh chives, to garnish

1 Cut the carrot, leek and celery into 2in long julienne strips. Slice the cabbage very finely.

NUTRITION NOTES

Per portion:	
Energy	69Kcals/288kJ
Protein	3.67g
Fat	0.71g
Saturated fat	0.05g
Fiber	2.82g

2 Put the stock and bay leaf into a large saucepan and bring to a boil. Add the carrot, leek and celery, cover and simmer for 6 minutes.

3 Add the cabbage, beans and pasta shapes. Stir, then simmer uncovered for another 4–5 minutes, or until the vegetables and pasta are tender.

4 Remove the bay leaf and season with salt and pepper to taste. Ladle into four soup bowls and garnish with chopped chives. Serve immediately.

CHICKEN AND PASTA SOUP

INGREDIENTS

Serves 4–6

3¾ cups chicken stock
1 bay leaf
4 scallions, sliced
8oz button mushrooms, sliced
4oz cooked chicken breast
2oz soup pasta
⅔ cup dry white wine
1 tablespoon chopped fresh parsley
salt and black pepper

NUTRITION NOTES

Per portion:

Energy	126Kcals/529kJ
Fat	2.2g
Saturated fat	0.6g
Cholesterol	19mg
Fiber	1.3g

1 Put the stock and bay leaf into a pan and bring to a boil.

2 Add the scallions and mushrooms to the stock.

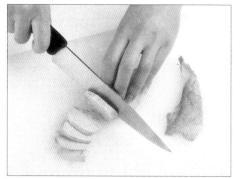

3 Remove the skin from the chicken and slice the meat thinly, using a sharp knife. Add to the soup and season to taste. Heat thoroughly for 2–3 minutes.

4 Add the pasta, cover and simmer for 7–8 minutes. Just before serving, add the wine and chopped parsley, reheat for 2–3 minutes, then season to taste.

Beet Soup with Ravioli

Serves 4–6

1 recipe basic pasta dough (see
   page 68)
egg white, beaten, for brushing
flour, for dusting
1 small onion or shallot, finely chopped
2 garlic cloves, crushed
1 tsp fennel seeds
2½ cups chicken stock
8oz cooked beets
2 tablespoons fresh orange juice
fennel or dill leaves, to garnish
crusty bread, to serve

For the filling

1½ cups finely chopped mushrooms
1 shallot or small onion, finely chopped
1–2 garlic cloves, crushed
1 tsp chopped fresh thyme
1 tbsp chopped fresh parsley
6 tbsp fresh white breadcrumbs
salt and black pepper
large pinch of ground nutmeg

1 Process all the filling ingredients in a food processor or blender.

NUTRITION NOTES	
Per portion:	
Energy	358Kcals/1504kJ
Fat	4.9g
Saturated fat	1.0g
Cholesterol	110mg
Fiber	4.3g

2 Roll the pasta dough into thin sheets. Lay one piece over a ravioli sheet and put a teaspoonful of the filling into each depression. Brush around the edges of each ravioli with egg white. Cover with another sheet of pasta, press the edges well together to seal and separate the individual shapes. Transfer to a floured dishtowel and let rest for 1 hour before cooking.

3 Cook the ravioli in a large pan of boiling salted water for 2 minutes, in batches, to keep them from sticking together. Remove and drop into a bowl of cold water for 5 seconds before placing on a tray. (You can make the pasta shapes a day in advance, if you like. Cover with plastic wrap and store in the fridge.)

4 Put the onion, garlic and fennel seeds into a pan with ⅔ cup of the stock. Bring to a boil, cover and simmer for 5 minutes until tender. Peel and finely dice the beets (reserve 4 tbsp for the garnish). Add the rest of the beets to the soup with the remaining stock and bring to a boil.

5 Add the orange juice and cooked ravioli and simmer for 2 minutes. Pour into shallow soup bowls and garnish with the reserved diced beets and fennel or dill leaves.

SPICY TOMATO AND LENTIL SOUP

INGREDIENTS

Serves 4

1 tbsp sunflower oil
1 onion, finely chopped
1–2 garlic cloves, crushed
1in piece fresh ginger, peeled and
    finely chopped
1 tsp cumin seeds, crushed
1 lb ripe tomatoes, peeled, seeded and
    chopped
½ cup red split lentils
5 cups vegetable or chicken stock
1 tbsp tomato paste
salt and black pepper
low fat plain yogurt and chopped fresh
    parsley, to garnish (optional)

1 Heat the sunflower oil in a large heavy saucepan and cook the chopped onion gently for 5 minutes, until softened.

2 Stir in the garlic, ginger and cumin, followed by the tomatoes and lentils. Cook over low heat for another 3–4 minutes.

3 Stir in the stock and tomato paste. Bring to a boil, then lower the heat and simmer gently for about 30 minutes, until the lentils are soft. Season to taste with salt and pepper.

4 Purée the soup in a blender or food processor. Return to the clean pan and reheat gently. Serve in heated bowls. If desired, garnish each portion with a swirl of yogurt and a little chopped parsley.

NUTRITION NOTES	
Per portion:	
Energy	165Kcals/695kJ
Fat	4g
Saturated fat	0.5g
Cholesterol	0

CREAMY COD CHOWDER

A delicious light version of a
classic, this chowder is a tasty
combination of smoked fish,
vegetables, fresh herbs and milk.
To cut the calories and stock
even more, use vegetable or fish
stock in place of the milk. Serve
as a substantial first course or
snack, or as a light main meal
accompanied by warm crusty
whole-wheat bread.

INGREDIENTS

Serves 4–6
12oz smoked cod fillet
1 small onion, finely chopped
1 bay leaf
4 black peppercorns
3¾ cups skim milk
2 tsp cornstarch
7oz canned corn
1 tbsp chopped fresh parsley

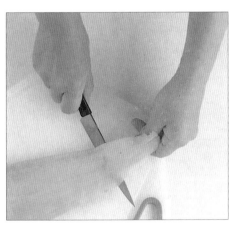

1 Skin the fish and put it into a large
saucepan with the onion, bay leaf
and peppercorns. Pour in the milk.

2 Bring to a boil, then reduce the
heat and simmer very gently for
12–15 minutes, or until the fish is just
cooked. Do not overcook.

3 Using a slotted spoon, lift out the
fish and flake into large chunks.
Remove the bay leaf and peppercorns
and discard.

4 Blend the cornstarch with 2 tsp cold
water and add to the pan. Bring to
a boil and simmer for 1 minute or until
slightly thickened.

5 Drain the corn and add to the
saucepan with the flaked fish and
parsley. Reheat gently and serve.

COOK'S TIP
The flavor of the chowder
improves if it is made a day in
advance. Allow to cool, then chill
until just before you plan to serve.
Reheat gently. Do not allow the
soup to boil, or the fish will
disintegrate.

NUTRITION NOTES

Per portion:
Energy	200Kcals/840kJ
Protein	24.71g
Fat	1.23g
Saturated fat	0.32g

SPINACH AND TOFU SOUP

This appetizing clear soup has an extremely delicate and mild flavor that can be used as a perfect counterbalance to the intense heat of a hot Thai curry.

INGREDIENTS

Serves 6
2 tbsp dried shrimp
4 cups chicken stock
8oz fresh tofu, drained and cut into
 ¾in cubes
2 tbsp fish sauce
12oz fresh spinach, washed
 thoroughly
black pepper
2 scallions, finely sliced, to garnish

1 Rinse and drain the dried shrimp. Combine the shrimp with the chicken stock in a large saucepan and bring to a boil.

2 Add the tofu and simmer for about 5 minutes. Season with fish sauce and black pepper to taste.

3 Tear the spinach leaves into bite-size pieces and add to the soup. Cook for another 1–2 minutes.

4 Remove from the heat and sprinkle with the finely sliced scallions, to garnish.

NUTRITION NOTES

Per portion:
Energy	64Kcals/270kJ
Fat	225g
Saturated fat	0.26g
Cholesterol	25mg
Fiber	1.28g

COOK'S TIP
Homemade chicken stock makes a world of difference to clear soups. Accumulate enough bones to make a big batch of stock, use what you need and keep the rest in the freezer.

Put 3–3½ pounds meaty chicken bones and 1 pound pork bones (optional) into a large saucepan. Add 12 cups water and slowly bring to a boil. Occasionally skim off and discard any scum that rises to the surface. Add 2 slices fresh ginger, 2 garlic cloves (optional), 2 celery stalks, 4 scallions, 2 bruised lemongrass stalks, a few sprigs of cilantro and 10 crushed black peppercorns. Reduce the heat to low and simmer for 2–2½ hours.

Remove from the heat and allow to cool, uncovered and undisturbed. Pour through a fine strainer, leaving the last dregs behind as they tend to cloud the soup. Allow to cool, then chill. Use as required, removing any fat that congeals on the surface.

VEGETABLE MINESTRONE

INGREDIENTS

Serves 6–8

large pinch of saffron strands
1 onion, chopped
1 leek, sliced
1 stalk celery, sliced
2 carrots, diced
2–3 garlic cloves, crushed
2½ cups chicken stock
28oz can chopped tomatoes
½ cup frozen peas
2oz soup pasta (anellini)
1 tsp sugar
1 tbsp chopped fresh parsley
1 tbsp chopped fresh basil
salt and black pepper

1 Soak the pinch of saffron strands in 1 tablespoon boiling water. Allow to stand for 10 minutes.

2 Meanwhile, put the prepared onion, leek, celery, carrots and garlic into a large pan. Add the chicken stock, bring to a boil, cover and simmer for about 10 minutes.

3 Add the canned tomatoes, the saffron with its liquid and the frozen peas. Bring back to a boil and add the soup pasta. Simmer for 10 minutes until tender.

COOK'S TIP
Saffron strands aren't essential for this soup, but they give a wonderfully delicate flavor, with the bonus of a lovely rich orange-yellow color.

4 Season with sugar, salt and pepper to taste. Stir in the chopped herbs just before serving.

NUTRITION NOTES	
Per portion:	
Energy	87Kcals/367kJ
Fat	0.7g
Saturated fat	0.1g
Cholesterol	0
Fiber	3.3g

Corn Chowder with Pasta Shells

Smoked turkey bacon provides a tasty, low fat alternative to bacon in this hearty dish. If you prefer, omit the meat altogether and serve the soup as is.

INGREDIENTS

Serves 4

1 small green bell pepper
1 lb potatoes, peeled and diced
2 cups canned or frozen corn
1 onion, chopped
1 celery stalk, chopped
a bouquet garni (bay leaf, parsley stalks and thyme)
2½ cups chicken stock
1¼ cups skim milk
2oz small pasta shells
oil, for frying
5oz smoked turkey bacon strips, diced
salt and black pepper
breadsticks, to serve

1 Halve the green pepper, then remove the stalk and seeds. Cut the flesh into small dice, cover with boiling water and let stand for 2 minutes. Drain and rinse.

NUTRITION NOTES

Per portion:

Energy	215Kcals/904kJ
Fat	1.6g
Saturated fat	0.3g
Cholesterol	13mg
Fiber	2.8g

2 Put the potatoes into a saucepan with the corn, onion, celery, green pepper, bouquet garni and stock. Bring to a boil, cover and simmer for 20 minutes, until tender.

3 Add the milk and season with salt and pepper. Process half the soup in a food processor or blender and return to the pan with the pasta shells. Simmer for 10 minutes.

4 Fry the turkey bacon in a nonstick frying pan for 2–3 minutes. Stir into the soup. Season to taste and serve with breadsticks.

CARROT AND CILANTRO SOUP

Nearly all root vegetables make excellent soups as they purée well and have an earthy flavor which complements the sharper flavors of herbs and spices. Carrots are particularly versatile, and this simple soup is elegant in both flavor and appearance.

INGREDIENTS

Serves 6

2 tsp sunflower oil
1 onion, chopped
1 celery stalk, sliced, plus 2–3 leafy
    celery tops
2 small potatoes, chopped
1 lb carrots, preferably young and
    tender, chopped
4 cups chicken stock
2–3 tsp ground coriander
1 tbsp chopped fresh cilantro
1 cup low-fat milk
salt and black pepper

1 Heat the oil in a large flameproof casserole or heavy saucepan and fry the onion over gentle heat for 3–4 minutes, until slightly softened but not browned. Add the celery and potato, cook for a few minutes, then add the carrot. Fry over gentle heat for 3–4 minutes, stirring frequently, and then cover. Reduce the heat even further and cook for about 10 minutes. Shake the pan or stir occasionally so the vegetables do not stick.

2 Add the stock, bring to a boil then partially cover and simmer for another 8–10 minutes, until the carrot and potato are tender.

3 Remove 6–8 tiny celery leaves for a garnish and finely chop about 1 tablespoon of the remaining celery tops. In a small saucepan, dry-fry the ground coriander for 1 minute, stirring constantly. Reduce the heat, add the chopped celery and cilantro and fry for about 1 minute. Set aside.

4 Process the soup in a food processor or blender and pour into a clean saucepan. Stir in the milk, coriander mixture and seasoning. Heat gently, taste and adjust the seasoning. Serve garnished with the reserved celery.

NUTRITION NOTES

Per portion:

Energy	76.5Kcals/320kJ
Fat	3.2g
Saturated fat	0.65g
Cholesterol	2.3mg
Fiber	2.2g

COOK'S TIP
For a more piquant flavor, add a little freshly squeezed lemon juice just before serving. The contrast between the orange-colored soup and the green garnish is a feast for the eyes as well as the taste buds.

CHICKEN AND COCONUT SOUP

This aromatic soup is rich with coconut milk and intensely flavored with galangal, lemongrass and kafir lime leaves.

INGREDIENTS

Serves 4–6

3 cups coconut milk
2 cups chicken stock
4 lemongrass stalks, bruised and chopped
1in section galangal, thinly sliced
10 black peppercorns, crushed
10 kafir lime leaves, torn
11oz boneless chicken, cut into thin strips
4oz button mushrooms
2oz canned baby corn
4 tbsp lime juice
about 3 tbsp fish sauce
2 fresh chilies, seeded and chopped, chopped scallions, and cilantro leaves, to garnish

1 Bring the coconut milk and chicken stock to a boil. Add the lemongrass, galangal, peppercorns and half the kafir lime leaves, reduce the heat and simmer gently for 10 minutes.

2 Strain the stock into a clean pan. Return to the heat, then add the chicken, button mushrooms and baby corn. Simmer for 5–7 minutes, or until the chicken is cooked.

3 Stir in the lime juice, fish sauce to taste and the rest of the lime leaves. Serve hot, garnished with chilies, scallions and cilantro.

NUTRITION NOTES	
Per portion:	
Energy	125Kcals/528kJ
Fat	3.03g
Saturated fat	1.06g
Cholesterol	32.5mg
Fiber	0.4g

HOT AND SOUR SHRIMP SOUP

This is a classic Thai seafood soup and is probably the most popular and well known soup from Thailand.

INGREDIENTS

Serves 4–6

1 lb jumbo shrimp
4 cups chicken stock
3 lemongrass stalks
10 kafir lime leaves, torn in half
8oz can straw mushrooms, drained
3 tbsp fish sauce
¼ cup lime juice
2 tbsp chopped scallions
1 tbsp cilantro leaves
4 fresh chilies, seeded and chopped
salt and black pepper

1 Shell and devein the shrimp and set aside. Rinse the shrimp shells, place them in a large saucepan with the stock and bring to a boil.

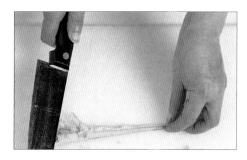

2 Bruise the lemongrass stalks with the blunt edge of a chopping knife and add them to the stock with half the lime leaves. Simmer gently for 5–6 minutes, until the stalks change color and the stock is fragrant.

NUTRITION NOTES	
Per portion:	
Energy	49Kcals/209kJ
Fat	0.45g
Saturated fat	0.07g
Cholesterol	78.8mg
Fiber	0.09g

3 Strain the stock, return to the saucepan and reheat. Add the mushrooms and shrimp, then cook until the shrimp turn pink. Stir in the fish sauce, lime juice, scallions, cilantro, chilies and the rest of the lime leaves. Taste the soup and adjust the seasoning – it should be sour, salty, spicy and hot.

RED ONION AND BEET SOUP

This beautiful, vivid ruby-red soup will look stunning at any dinner party.

INGREDIENTS

Serves 6
2 tsp olive oil
12oz red onions, sliced
2 garlic cloves, crushed
10oz cooked beets,
   cut into sticks
5 cups vegetable stock
   or water
1 cup cooked soup pasta
2 tbsp raspberry vinegar
salt and black pepper
low fat yogurt and chopped chives,
   to garnish

COOK'S TIP
If you prefer, try substituting cooked barley for the pasta to give extra nuttiness.

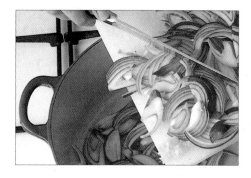

1 Heat the olive oil and add the onions and garlic.

2 Cook gently for about 20 minutes or until soft and tender.

3 Add the beets, stock or water, cooked pasta shapes and vinegar and heat thoroughly.

4 Adjust the seasoning to taste. Ladle the soup into bowls. Top each one with a spoonful of yogurt and sprinkle with chopped chives. Serve piping hot.

NUTRITION NOTES	
Per portion:	
Energy	76Kcals/318kJ
Fat	2.01g
Saturated fat	0.28g
Cholesterol	0.33mg
Fiber	1.83g

CAULIFLOWER AND BEAN SOUP

The sweet, licorice flavor of the fennel seeds gives a delicious edge to this hearty soup.

INGREDIENTS

Serves 6

2 tsp olive oil
1 garlic clove, crushed
1 onion, chopped
2 tsp fennel seeds
1 cauliflower, cut into small florets
2 x 14oz cans small cannellini beans,
* drained and rinsed*
5 cups vegetable stock
* or water*
salt and black pepper
chopped fresh parsley, to garnish
toasted slices of French bread, to serve

1 Heat the olive oil. Add the garlic, onion and fennel seeds and cook gently for 5 minutes or until the onion is softened.

2 Add the cauliflower, half of the beans and all the stock or water.

3 Bring to a boil. Reduce the heat and simmer for 10 minutes or until the cauliflower is tender.

NUTRITION NOTES

Per portion:

Energy	194.3Kcals/822.5kJ
Fat	3.41g
Saturated fat	0.53g
Cholesterol	0
Fiber	7.85g

4 Pour the soup into a blender and blend until smooth. Stir in the remaining beans and season to taste. Reheat and pour into bowls. Sprinkle with chopped parsley and serve with toasted slices of French bread.

MELON AND BASIL SOUP

A deliciously refreshing, chilled fruit soup, just right for a hot summer's day. It takes next to no time to prepare, leaving you free to enjoy the sunshine and, even better, it is almost totally fat-free.

INGREDIENTS

Serves 4–6
2 cantaloupes
6 tbsp sugar
¾ cup water
finely grated rind and juice of 1 lime
3 tablespoons shredded fresh basil
fresh basil leaves, to garnish

1 Cut the melons in half across the middle. Scrape out the seeds and discard. Using a melon baller, scoop out 20–24 balls and set aside for the garnish. Scoop out the remaining flesh and place in a blender or food processor. Set aside.

2 Place the sugar, water and lime zest in a small pan over low heat. Stir until dissolved, bring to a boil and simmer for 2–3 minutes. Remove from the heat and allow to cool slightly. Pour half the mixture into the blender or food processor with the melon flesh. Blend until smooth, adding the remaining syrup and lime juice to taste.

3 Pour the mixture into a bowl, stir in the basil and chill. Serve garnished with basil leaves and melon balls.

NUTRITION NOTES

Per portion:

Energy	69Kcals/293.8kJ
Fat	0.14g
Saturated fat	0
Cholesterol	0
Fiber	0.47g

COOK'S TIP
Add the syrup in two stages, because the amount of sugar needed will depend on the sweetness of the melon.

CHILLED FRESH TOMATO SOUP

This effortless uncooked soup can be made in minutes.

INGREDIENTS

Serves 6
3–3½ lb ripe tomatoes, peeled and
  coarsely chopped
4 garlic cloves, crushed
2 tbsp balsamic vinegar
4 thick slices whole-wheat bread
black pepper
low fat ricotta cheese, to garnish

1 Place the tomatoes in a blender with the garlic. Blend until smooth.

2 Press the mixture through a sieve to remove the seeds. Stir in the balsamic vinegar and season to taste with pepper. Put in the fridge to chill.

3 Toast the bread lightly on both sides. While still hot, cut off the crusts and slice the toast in half horizontally. Place on a board with the uncooked sides facing down and, using a circular motion, rub to remove any doughy pieces of bread.

COOK'S TIP
For the best flavor, it is important to use only fully-ripened, flavorful tomatoes in this soup.

4 Cut each slice into four triangles. Place on a broiler pan and toast the uncooked sides until lightly golden. Garnish each bowl of soup with a spoonful of ricotta cheese and serve with the Melba toast.

NUTRITION NOTES	
Per portion:	
Energy	111Kcals/475kJ
Fat	1.42g
Saturated fat	0.39g
Cholesterol	0.16mg
Fiber	4.16g

APPETIZERS AND SNACKS

Healthy low fat appetizers provide a delicious start to a meal and are quick and easy to make. Appetizers should not be too filling because they are simply setting the scene for the low fat main course to follow. Choose from a tempting selection of recipes, including light and refreshing fruit cocktails such as Minted Melon and Grapefruit and vegetable pâtés or dips such as Guacamole with Crudités. Quick and easy snacks and light dishes are ideal served with thick slices of warm, crusty bread for a low fat, nutritious lunch or supper. We include a selection of tasty snacks, such as Pasta with Herb Scallops, Cheese and Chutney Toasts and Prosciutto and Pepper Pizzas.

MELON, PINEAPPLE AND GRAPE COCKTAIL

A light, refreshing fruit salad, with no added sugar and virtually no fat, perfect for breakfast or brunch – or any time.

INGREDIENTS

Serves 4

½ melon
8oz fresh or canned pineapple packed in juice
8oz seedless white grapes, halved
½ cup white grape juice
fresh mint leaves, to decorate (optional)

1 Remove the seeds from the melon half and use a melon baller to scoop out even-size balls.

COOK'S TIP
A melon is ready to eat when it smells sweet even through its thick skin. Use a firm-fleshed fruit, such as a cantaloupe or honeydew melon.

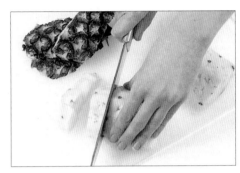

2 Using a sharp knife, cut the skin from the pineapple and discard. Cut the fruit into bite-size chunks.

3 Combine all the fruits in a glass serving dish and add the grape juice. If you are using canned pineapple, measure the drained juice and bring it up to the required quantity with the grape juice.

4 If not serving immediately, cover and chill. Serve decorated with mint leaves, if desired.

NUTRITION NOTES

Per portion:

Energy	95Kcals/395kJ
Fat	0.5g
Saturated fat	0
Cholesterol	0

GRAPEFRUIT SALAD WITH ORANGE

The bittersweet flavor of Campari combines especially well with citrus fruit. Because of its alcohol content, this dish is not suitable for children.

INGREDIENTS

Serves 4
3 tbsp sugar
4 tbsp Campari
2 tbsp lemon juice
4 grapefruits
5 oranges
4 sprigs fresh mint

NUTRITION NOTES

Per portion:	
Energy	196Kcals/822kJ
Fat	5.9g
Saturated fat	2.21g
Cholesterol	66.37mg
Fiber	1.6g

1 Bring ²/₃ cup water to a boil in a small saucepan, add the sugar and simmer until dissolved. Allow to cool, then add the Campari and lemon juice. Chill until ready to serve.

COOK'S TIP
When buying citrus fruit, choose brightly colored specimens that feel heavy for their size.

2 Cut the peel from the grapefruit and oranges with a serrated knife. Segment the fruit into a bowl by slipping a small paring knife between the flesh and the membranes. Combine the fruit with the Campari syrup and chill.

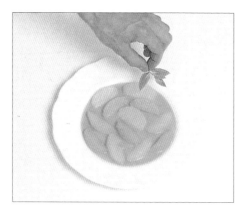

3 Spoon the salad into four dishes and garnish each dish with a sprig of fresh mint.

MINTED MELON AND GRAPEFRUIT

Melon is always a popular appetizer. Here the succulent flavor of the cantaloupe is complemented by the refreshing taste of citrus fruit and a simple mustard and vinegar dressing. Fresh mint, used in the cocktail and as a garnish, enhances both its flavor and appearance.

INGREDIENTS

Serves 4

1 cantaloupe, weighing about
   2¼lb
2 pink grapefruit
1 yellow grapefruit
1 tsp Dijon mustard
1 tsp raspberry or sherry vinegar
1 tsp honey
1 tbsp chopped fresh mint
a few sprigs of fresh mint,
   to garnish

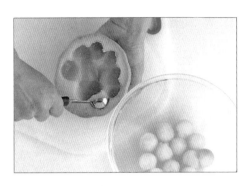

1 Halve the melon and remove the seeds with a teaspoon. With a melon baller, carefully scoop the flesh into balls.

NUTRITION NOTES

Per portion:	
Energy	97Kcals/409kJ
Protein	2.22g
Fat	0.63g
Saturated fat	0
Fiber	3.05g

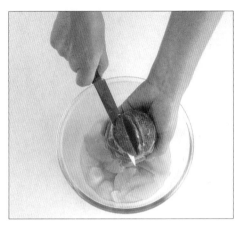

2 With a small sharp knife, peel the grapefruit and remove all the white pith. Remove the segments by cutting between the membranes, holding the fruit over a small bowl to catch any juices.

3 Whisk the mustard, vinegar, honey, chopped mint and grapefruit juices together in a mixing bowl. Add the melon balls and the grapefruit and mix well. Chill for 30 minutes.

4 Ladle the fruit into four glass dishes and serve garnished with sprigs of fresh mint.

GUACAMOLE WITH CRUDITÉS

This fresh-tasting spicy dip is made using peas instead of the avocados that are traditionally associated with this dish. This version saves on both fat and calories, without compromising taste.

INGREDIENTS

Serves 4–6

2¼ cups frozen peas, defrosted
1 garlic clove, crushed
2 scallions, chopped
1 tsp finely grated rind and juice of 1 lime
½ tsp ground cumin
dash of Tabasco sauce
1 tbsp reduced-fat mayonnaise
2 tbsp chopped cilantro or parsley
salt and black pepper
pinch of paprika and lime slices, to garnish

For the crudités

6 baby carrots
2 celery stalks
1 red-skinned eating apple
1 pear
1 tbsp lemon or lime juice
6 canned baby corns

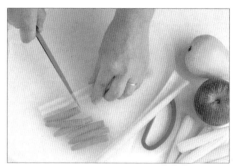

1 Put the peas, garlic clove, scallions, lime rind and juice, cumin, Tabasco sauce, mayonnaise and salt and black pepper into a food processor or a blender for a few minutes and process until smooth.

2 Add the chopped cilantro or parsley and process for a few more seconds. Spoon into a serving bowl, cover with plastic wrap and chill in the fridge for 30 minutes, to let the flavors develop fully.

3 For the crudités, trim and peel the carrots. Halve the celery stalks lengthwise and trim into sticks, the same length as the carrots. Quarter, core and thickly slice the apple and pear, then dip into the lemon or lime juice. Arrange with the baby corn on a platter.

4 Sprinkle the paprika over the guacamole and garnish with twisted lime slices.

NUTRITION NOTES

Per portion:	
Energy	110Kcals/460kJ
Protein	6.22g
Fat	2.29g
Saturated fat	0.49g
Fiber	6.73g

COOK'S TIP
Serve the guacamole with warmed whole-wheat pita bread.

TZATZIKI

Tzatziki is a Greek cucumber salad dressed with yogurt, mint and garlic. It is typically served with grilled lamb and chicken, but is also good served with crudités.

INGREDIENTS

Serves 4
1 cucumber
1 tsp salt
3 tbsp finely chopped fresh mint, plus a
    few sprigs to garnish
1 garlic clove, crushed
1 tsp sugar
1 cup low fat plain yogurt
cucumber flower, to garnish (optional)

COOK'S TIP
If you want to prepare Tzatziki in a hurry, then leave out the method for salting cucumber at the end of step 1. The cucumber will have a more crunchy texture, and will be slightly less sweet.

1 Peel the cucumber. Reserve a little of the cucumber to use as a garnish if desired and cut the rest in half lengthwise. Remove the seeds with a teaspoon and discard. Slice the cucumber thinly and combine with salt. Let stand for 15–20 minutes. Salt will soften the cucumber and draw out any bitter juices.

2 Combine the mint, garlic, sugar and yogurt in a bowl, reserving a few sprigs of mint as decoration.

3 Rinse the cucumber in a sieve under cold running water to remove the salt. Drain well and combine with the yogurt. Decorate with cucumber flower and/or mint. Serve cold.

NUTRITION NOTES

Per portion:
Energy	41.5Kcals/174.5kJ
Fat	0.51g
Saturated fat	0.25g
Cholesterol	2mg
Fiber	0.2g

CHILI TOMATO SALSA

This universal dip is great served with absolutely anything and can be made up to 24 hours in advance.

INGREDIENTS

Serves 4

1 shallot, peeled and halved
2 garlic cloves, peeled
handful of fresh basil leaves
1¼ lb ripe tomatoes
2 tsp olive oil
2 green chilies
salt and black pepper

1 Place the shallot and garlic in a food processor with the fresh basil. Blend the shallot, garlic and basil until finely chopped.

2 Halve the tomatoes and add to the food processor. Pulse the machine until the mixture is well blended and coarsely chopped.

3 With the motor running, slowly pour in the olive oil. Add salt and pepper to taste.

NUTRITION NOTES	
Per portion:	
Energy	28Kcals/79kJ
Fat	0.47g
Saturated fat	0.13g
Cholesterol	0
Fiber	1.45g

4 Halve the chilies lengthwise and remove the seeds. Finely slice the chilies across the width into tiny strips and stir into the tomato salsa. Serve at room temperature.

COOK'S TIP
The salsa is best made in the summer when tomatoes are at their best. In winter, use a drained 14oz can of plum tomatoes.

MELON WITH WILD STRAWBERRIES

This fragrant, colorful first course is the perfect way to begin a rich meal, because both melons and strawberries are virtually fat-free. Here several varieties of melon are combined with strongly flavored wild or woodland strawberries. If wild strawberries are not available, use ordinary strawberries or raspberries.

INGREDIENTS

Serves 4
1 cantaloupe
1 honeydew melon
2 lb watermelon
6oz wild strawberries
4 sprigs fresh mint, to garnish

NUTRITION NOTES

Per portion:
Energy	42.5Kcals/178.6kJ
Fat	0.32g
Saturated fat	0
Cholesterol	0
Fiber	1.09g

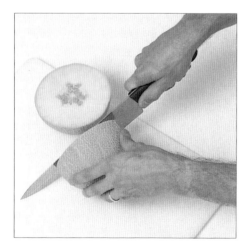

1 Using a large sharp knife, cut all three melons in half.

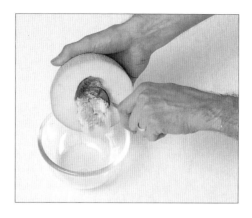

2 Scoop out the seeds from both the cantaloupe and honeydew melon with a spoon.

3 With a melon scoop, take out as many balls as you can from all three melons. Combine in a large bowl and chill for at least 1 hour.

4 Add the wild strawberries and mix together gently. Spoon out into four stemmed glass dishes.

5 Garnish each of the melon salads with a small sprig of mint and serve immediately.

COOK'S TIP
Ripe melons should give slightly when pressed at the base, and should give off a sweet scent. Buy carefully if you plan to use the fruit on the same day. If one or more varieties of melon aren't available, then substitute another, or buy two or three of the same variety – the salad might not be quite so colorful, but it will taste equally refreshing.

MUSSELS WITH THAI HERBS

Another simple dish to prepare. The lemongrass adds a refreshing tang to the mussels.

Serves 6

2¼ lb mussels, *cleaned and beards removed*
2 lemongrass stalks, *finely chopped*
4 shallots, *chopped*
4 kafir lime leaves, *coarsely torn*
2 red chilies, *sliced*
1 tbsp fish sauce
2 tbsp lime juice
2 scallions, *chopped, and cilantro leaves, to garnish*

1 Put all the ingredients, except the scallions and cilantro, in a large saucepan and stir thoroughly.

2 Cover and cook for 5–7 minutes, shaking the saucepan occasionally, until the mussels open. Discard any mussels that do not open.

3 Transfer the cooked mussels to a serving platter.

4 Garnish the mussels with chopped scallions and cilantro leaves. Serve immediately.

NUTRITION NOTES	
Per portion:	
Energy	56Kcals/238kJ
Fat	1.22g
Saturated fat	0.16g
Cholesterol	0.32mg
Fiber	27g

PASTA WITH HERBED SCALLOPS

Low-fat ricotta cheese, flavored
with mustard, garlic and herbs,
makes a deceptively creamy
sauce for pasta.

INGREDIENTS

Serves 4

½ cup low-fat ricotta cheese
2 tsp whole-grain mustard
2 garlic cloves, crushed
2–3 tbsp fresh lime juice
4 tbsp chopped fresh parsley
2 tbsp chopped chives
12oz black tagliatelle
12 large bay scallops
4 tbsp white wine
⅔ cup fish stock
salt and black pepper
lime wedges and parsley sprigs,
  to garnish

1 To make the sauce, combine the
ricotta cheese, mustard, garlic, lime
juice, parsley, chives and seasoning in a
mixing bowl.

2 Cook the pasta in a large pot of
boiling salted water until *al dente*.
Drain thoroughly.

3 Slice the scallops in half horizontally. Put the wine and fish stock into
a saucepan and heat to simmering
point. Add the scallops and cook very
gently for 3–4 minutes at the most.
(Don't cook any longer, or they
will toughen.)

COOK'S TIP
Black tagliatelle, made with squid
ink, is available from Italian deli-
catessens, but other colors can be
used to make this dish – try a
mixture of white and green.

4 Remove the scallops. Boil the wine
and stock to reduce by half and add
the green sauce to the pan. Heat gently
to warm, then return the scallops to the
pan and cook for 1 minute. Spoon onto
the pasta and garnish with lime wedges
and parsley.

NUTRITION NOTES	
Per portion:	
Energy	368Kcals/1561kJ
Fat	4.01g
Saturated fat	0.98g
Cholesterol	99mg
Fiber	1.91g

FRESH FIG, APPLE AND DATE SALAD

Sweet Mediterranean figs and dates combine especially well with crisp eating apples. A hint of almond serves to unite the flavors, but if you'd prefer to reduce the fat even more, omit the almond paste and add another 2 tablespoons low fat plain yogurt or use low fat ricotta cheese instead.

INGREDIENTS

Serves 4
6 large eating apples
juice of ½ lemon
6oz fresh dates
1oz almond paste
1 tsp orange-flower water
4 tbsp low fat plain yogurt
4 green or purple figs
4 almonds, toasted

1 Core the apples. Slice thinly, then cut into fine matchsticks. Moisten with lemon juice to keep them white.

NUTRITION NOTES

Per portion:
Energy	255Kcals/876.5kJ
Fat	4.98g
Saturated fat	505g
Cholesterol	2.25mg
Fiber	1.69g

2 Remove the pits from the dates and cut the flesh into fine strips, then combine with the apple slices.

3 Soften the almond paste with orange-flower water and combine with the yogurt. Mix well.

COOK'S TIP
For a slightly stronger almond flavor, add a few drops of almond extract to the yogurt mixture. When buying fresh figs, choose firm, unblemished fruit which give slightly when lightly squeezed. Avoid damaged, bruised or very soft fruit.

4 Pile the apples and dates in the center of four plates. Remove the stem from each of the figs and divide the fruit into quarters without cutting through the base. Squeeze the base with the thumb and forefinger of each hand to open up the fruit.

5 Place a fig in the center of each salad. Spoon the yogurt filling onto the figs and decorate each one with a toasted almond.

Cheese and Chutney Toasts

Quick cheese on toast can be made quite memorable with a few tasty additions. Serve these scrumptious toasts with a simple lettuce and cherry tomato salad.

Ingredients

Serves 4
4 slices whole-wheat bread
3½oz Cheddar cheese, grated
1 tsp dried thyme
2 tbsp chutney or relish
black pepper
salad, to serve

1 Toast the bread slices lightly on each side.

2 Combine the cheese and thyme and season to taste with pepper.

Nutrition Notes

Per portion:
Energy	157.25Kcals/664.25kJ
Fat	4.24g
Saturated fat	1.99g
Cholesterol	9.25mg
Fiber	2.41g

4 Return the toast to the broiler and cook until the cheese is browned and bubbling. Cut each slice in half, diagonally, and serve immediately with salad.

Cook's Tip
If you prefer, use a reduced fat hard cheese, such as aged Cheddar or Gruyère, in place of the full-fat Cheddar to cut both calories and fat.

3 Spread the chutney or relish on the toast and divide the cheese evenly among the four slices.

PROSCIUTTO AND PEPPER PIZZAS

The delicious flavors of these easy pizzas are hard to beat.

INGREDIENTS

Makes 4

½ loaf crusty Italian bread
1 red bell pepper, roasted and peeled
1 yellow bell pepper, roasted and
  peeled
4 slices prosciutto, cut into
  thick strips
2oz reduced fat mozzarella cheese
black pepper

NUTRITION NOTES

Per portion:

Energy	93Kcals/395kJ
Fat	3.25g
Saturated fat	1.49g
Cholesterol	14mg
Fiber	1g

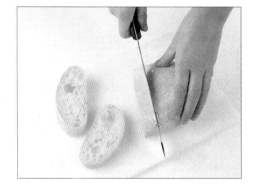

1 Cut the bread into four thick slices and toast until golden.

2 Cut the roasted peppers into thick strips and arrange on the toasted bread with the strips of prosciutto. Preheat the broiler.

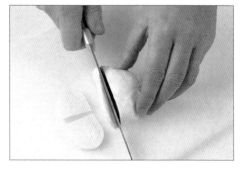

3 Thinly slice the mozzarella and arrange on top, then grind over plenty of black pepper. Broil for 2–3 minutes, until the cheese is bubbling.

4 Sprinkle the basil leaves on top and serve immediately.

PASTA, BEANS AND GRAINS

Pasta on its own is low in fat and is a good source of carbohydrates, but it is often served with heavy high fat sauces. This food is very versatile, and sauces do not need to be high in fat to be appetizing. Pasta and pizzas are always a popular choice at mealtimes, and all that taste with very little fat makes these recipes a delicious and nutritious option. From French bread pizzas to pasta served with tasty meat, vegetable or fish sauces, including old favorites like Spaghetti Bolognese, these recipes are sure to satisfy those pangs of hunger every time.

Macaroni and Cheese with Turkey

A tasty low fat alternative to macaroni and cheese, the addition of smoked turkey bacon makes this dish a family favorite. Serve with warm Italian bread and a mixed green salad.

NUTRITION NOTES	
Per portion:	
Energy	152Kcals/637kJ
Fat	2.8g
Saturated fat	0.7g
Cholesterol	12mg
Fiber	1.1g

INGREDIENTS

Serves 4

1 medium onion, chopped
⅔ cup vegetable or chicken stock
2 tbsp low fat margarine
3 tbsp all-purpose flour
¼ cup skim milk
2oz reduced fat Cheddar cheese, grated
1 tsp dry mustard
8oz macaroni
4 turkey bacon strips, cut in half
2–3 firm tomatoes, sliced
a few fresh basil leaves
1 tbsp grated Parmesan cheese
salt and black pepper

2 Put the margarine, flour, milk and seasoning into a saucepan and whisk together over the heat until thickened and smooth. Set aside and add the cheese, mustard and onion.

1 Put the chopped onion and stock into a nonstick frying pan. Bring to a boil, stirring occasionally, and cook for 5–6 minutes or until the stock has reduced entirely and the onion is transparent.

3 Cook the macaroni in a large pot of boiling, salted water according to the instructions on the package. Preheat the broiler. Drain the macaroni thoroughly and stir into the sauce. Transfer to a shallow ovenproof dish.

4 Arrange the turkey bacon and tomatoes overlapping on top of the macaroni and cheese. Tuck in the basil leaves, then sprinkle with Parmesan and broil to lightly brown the top.

PASTA WITH TOMATO AND TUNA

INGREDIENTS

Serves 6

1 medium onion, finely chopped
1 celery stalk, finely chopped
1 red bell pepper, seeded and diced
1 garlic clove, crushed
⅔ cup chicken stock
1 14oz can chopped tomatoes
1 tbsp tomato paste
2 tsp sugar
1 tbsp chopped fresh basil
1 tbsp chopped fresh parsley
1 lb pasta shells
1 14oz can tuna, drained
2 tbsp capers in vinegar, drained
salt and black pepper

1 Put the chopped onion, celery, red pepper and garlic into a nonstick pan. Add the stock, bring to a boil and cook for 5 minutes or until the stock has reduced almost completely.

2 Add the tomatoes, tomato paste, sugar and herbs. Season to taste and bring to a boil. Simmer for about 30 minutes, until thick, stirring occasionally.

3 Meanwhile, cook the pasta in a large pot of boiling, salted water according to the package instructions, until *al dente*. Drain thoroughly and transfer to a warm serving dish.

COOK'S TIP
If fresh herbs are not available, use a 14oz can of chopped tomatoes with herbs and add 1–2 tsp mixed dried herbs, in place of the fresh herbs.

4 Flake the tuna into large chunks and add to the sauce with the capers. Heat gently for 1–2 minutes, pour over the pasta, toss and serve immediately.

NUTRITION NOTES

Per portion:

Energy	369Kcals/1549kJ
Fat	2.1g
Saturated fat	0.4g
Cholesterol	34mg
Fiber	4g

CRAB PASTA SALAD

Low fat yogurt makes a piquant dressing for this salad.

INGREDIENTS

Serves 6

12oz pasta twists
1 small red bell pepper, seeded and
  finely chopped
2 6oz cans white crabmeat, drained
4oz cherry tomatoes, halved
¼ cucumber, halved, seeded and sliced
  into crescents
1 tbsp lemon juice
1¼ cups low fat yogurt
2 celery stalks, finely chopped
2 tsp creamed horseradish
½ tsp paprika
½ tsp Dijon mustard
2 tbsp sweet tomato pickle
  or chutney
salt and black pepper
fresh basil, to garnish

1 Cook the pasta in a large pot of boiling, salted water, according to the instructions on the package, until *al dente*. Drain and rinse thoroughly under cold water.

NUTRITION NOTES	
Per portion:	
Energy	305Kcals/1283kJ
Fat	2.5g
Saturated fat	0.5g
Cholesterol	43mg
Fiber	2.9g

2 Cover the chopped red pepper with boiling water and allow to stand for 1 minute. Drain and rinse under cold water. Pat dry with paper towels.

3 Drain the crabmeat and pick over carefully for pieces of shell. Put into a bowl with the halved tomatoes and sliced cucumber. Season with salt and pepper and sprinkle with lemon juice.

4 To make the dressing, add the red pepper to the yogurt, with the celery, creamed horseradish, paprika, mustard and sweet tomato pickle or chutney. Mix the pasta with the dressing and transfer to a serving dish. Spoon the crab mixture on top and garnish with fresh basil.

FUSILLI WITH SMOKED TROUT

INGREDIENTS

Serves 4–6

2 carrots, julienned
1 leek, julienned
2 celery stalks, julienned
⅔ cup vegetable or fish stock
8oz smoked trout fillets, skinned and
  cut into strips
7oz low fat cream cheese
⅔ cup medium-sweet white wine or
  fish stock
1 tbsp chopped fresh dill
  or fennel
8oz fusilli (long, corkscrew pasta)
salt and black pepper
dill sprigs, to garnish

1 Put the carrots, leek and celery into
a pan with the vegetable stock.
Bring to a boil and cook quickly for
4–5 minutes, until the vegetables are
tender and most of the stock has evaporated. Remove from the heat
and add the smoked trout.

2 To make the sauce, put the low fat
cream cheese and wine into a
saucepan, heat and whisk until smooth.
Season with salt and pepper. Add the
chopped dill.

3 Cook the pasta according to the
package instructions in a large pot
of boiling, salted water until al dente.
Drain thoroughly.

4 Return the pasta to the pan with
the sauce, toss lightly and transfer
to a serving bowl. Top with the cooked
vegetables and trout. Serve at once,
garnished with dill sprigs.

NUTRITION NOTES

Per portion:

Energy	339Kcals/1422kJ
Fat	4.7g
Saturated fat	0.8g
Cholesterol	57mg
Fiber	4.1g

COOK'S TIP
When making the sauce, it is
important to whisk it continuously while heating, to ensure a
smooth result. Smoked salmon
may be used in place of the trout,
for a tasty change.

Hot Spicy Shrimp with Pasta

This low fat shrimp sauce tossed with hot pasta is an ideal supper-time dish. Add less or more chili depending on how hot you like your food.

Ingredients

Serves 4–6

8oz large shrimp, cooked
   and peeled
1–2 garlic cloves, crushed
finely grated rind of 1 lemon
1 tbsp lemon juice
¼ tsp red chili paste or 1 large pinch of
   chili powder
1 tbsp light soy sauce
5oz smoked turkey bacon strips
1 shallot or small onion, finely chopped
4 tbsp dry white wine
8oz campanelle or other pasta shapes
4 tbsp fish stock
4 firm ripe tomatoes, peeled, seeded
   and chopped
2 tbsp chopped fresh parsley
salt and black pepper

Nutrition Notes

Per portion:

Energy	331Kcals/1388kJ
Fat	2.9g
Saturated fat	0.6g
Cholesterol	64mg
Fiber	3.2g

Cook's Tip

To save time later, the shrimp and marinade ingredients can be mixed together, covered and chilled in the fridge overnight, until ready to use.

1 In a glass bowl, mix the shrimp with the garlic, lemon rind and juice, chili paste and soy sauce. Season with salt and pepper, cover and marinate for at least 1 hour.

2 Broil the turkey bacon strips, then cut them into ¼ in dice.

3 Put the shallot or onion and white wine into a pan, bring to a boil, cover and cook for 2–3 minutes, or until they are tender and the wine has reduced by half.

4 Cook the pasta according to the package instructions in a large pot of boiling, salted water until al dente. Drain thoroughly.

5 Just before serving, put the shrimp with its marinade into a large frying pan, bring to a boil quickly and add the smoked turkey bacon and fish stock. Heat thoroughly for 1 minute.

6 Add to the pasta with the chopped tomatoes and parsley, toss quickly and serve immediately.

TAGLIATELLE WITH MUSHROOMS

INGREDIENTS

Serves 4

1 small onion, finely chopped
2 garlic cloves, crushed
⅔ cup vegetable stock
8oz mixed fresh mushrooms, such as
   portobello, oyster or chanterelles
4 tbsp white or red wine
2 tsp tomato paste
1 tbsp soy sauce
1 tsp chopped fresh thyme
2 tbsp chopped fresh parsley, plus extra
   to garnish
8oz fresh sun-dried tomato and herb
   tagliatelle
salt and black pepper
shavings of Parmesan cheese, to serve
   (optional)

1 Put the onion and garlic into a pan with the stock, then cover and cook for 5 minutes or until tender.

2 Add the mushrooms (quartered or sliced if large or left whole if small), wine, tomato paste and soy sauce. Cover and cook for 5 minutes.

NUTRITION NOTES	
Per portion:	
Energy	241Kcals/1010kJ
Fat	2.4g
Saturated fat	0.7g
Carbohydrate	45g
Fiber	3g

3 Remove the lid from the pan and boil until the liquid has reduced by half. Stir in the chopped fresh herbs and season to taste.

4 Cook the fresh pasta in a large pot of boiling, salted water for 2–5 minutes, until *al dente*. Drain thoroughly and toss lightly with the mushrooms. Serve, garnished with parsley and shavings of Parmesan cheese, if desired.

PASTA PRIMAVERA

You can use any mixture of fresh, young spring vegetables to make this delicately flavored pasta dish.

INGREDIENTS

8oz thin asparagus spears, chopped in half
4oz snow peas, ends removed
4oz canned baby corn or fresh corn kernels
8oz whole baby carrots, trimmed
1 small red bell pepper, seeded and chopped
8 scallions, sliced
8oz torchietti or other pasta shapes
⅔ cup low fat cottage cheese
⅔ cup low fat yogurt
1 tbsp lemon juice
1 tbsp chopped parsley
1 tbsp chopped chives
skim milk (optional)
salt and black pepper
sun-dried tomato bread, to serve

1 Cook the asparagus spears in a pan of boiling, salted water for 3–4 minutes. Add the snow peas halfway through the cooking time. Drain and rinse both under cold water to stop further cooking.

2 Cook the corn, carrots, red pepper and scallions in the same way until tender. Drain and rinse.

3 Cook the pasta in a large pot of boiling, salted water according to the packet instruction, until *al dente*. Drain thoroughly.

4 Put the cottage cheese, yogurt, lemon juice, parsley, chives and seasoning into a food processor or blender and process until smooth. Thin the sauce with skim milk, if necessary. Put into a large pan with the pasta and vegetables, heat gently and toss carefully. Serve immediately with sun-dried tomato bread.

NUTRITION NOTES

Per portion:

Energy	320Kcals/1344kJ
Fat	3.1g
Saturated fat	0.4g
Cholesterol	3mg
Fiber	6.2g

TAGLIATELLE WITH MILANESE SAUCE

INGREDIENTS

Serves 4

1 onion, *finely chopped*
1 celery stalk, *finely chopped*
1 red bell pepper, *seeded and diced*
1–2 garlic cloves, *crushed*
⅔ cup vegetable or chicken stock
1 14oz can tomatoes
1 tbsp tomato paste
2 tsp sugar
1 tsp mixed dried herbs
12oz tagliatelle
1½ cups sliced button mushrooms
4 tbsp dry white wine
4oz lean cooked ham, *diced*
salt and black pepper
1 tbsp chopped fresh parsley,
    to garnish

1 Put the chopped onion, celery, pepper and garlic into a saucepan. Add the stock, bring to a boil and cook for 5 minutes or until tender.

COOK'S TIP

To reduce the calorie and fat content even more, omit the ham and use corn kernels or cooked broccoli florets instead.

2 Add the tomatoes, tomato paste, sugar and herbs. Season with salt and pepper. Bring to a boil and simmer for 30 minutes, stirring occasionally, until the sauce is thick.

3 Cook the pasta in a large pot of boiling, salted water according to the package instructions, until *al dente*. Drain thoroughly.

4 Put the mushrooms into a pan with the white wine, cover and cook for 3–4 minutes, until the mushrooms are tender and all the wine has been absorbed.

5 Stir the mushrooms and ham into the tomato sauce and reheat gently over low heat.

6 Transfer the pasta to a warmed serving dish and spoon on the sauce. Garnish with parsley.

NUTRITION NOTES

Per portion:

Energy	405Kcals/1700kJ
Fat	3.5g
Saturated fat	0.8g
Cholesterol	17mg
Fiber	4.5g

SPAGHETTI WITH CHILI BEAN SAUCE

A nutritious vegetarian option, ideal as a low-fat main course.

INGREDIENTS

Serves 6

1 onion, finely chopped
1–2 garlic cloves, crushed
1 large green chili, seeded
  and chopped
⅔ cup vegetable stock
1 14oz can chopped tomatoes
2 tbsp tomato paste
½ cup red wine
1 tsp dried oregano
7 ounces green beans, sliced
1 14oz can red kidney
  beans, drained
1 14oz can cannellini
  beans, drained
1 14oz can chickpeas, drained
1 lb spaghetti
salt and black pepper

NUTRITION NOTES	
Per portion:	
Energy	431Kcals/1811kJ
Fat	3.6g
Saturated fat	0.2g
Cholesterol	0
Fiber	9.9g

2 Add the tomatoes, tomato paste, wine, seasoning and oregano. Bring to a boil, cover and simmer the sauce for 20 minutes.

3 Cook the green beans in boiling, salted water for about 5–6 minutes, until tender. Drain thoroughly.

1 To make the sauce, put the chopped onion, garlic and chili into a non-stick pan with the stock. Bring to a boil and cook for 5 minutes, until tender.

4 Add all the beans and the chickpeas to the sauce and simmer for another 10 minutes. Meanwhile, cook the spaghetti in a large pot of boiling, salted water according to the individual package instructions, until *al dente*. Drain thoroughly. Transfer the pasta to a serving dish or plates and top with the chili bean sauce.

> **COOK'S TIP**
> Rinse canned beans thoroughly under cold, running water to remove as much salt as possible, and drain well before use.

PINEAPPLE AND GINGER NOODLE SALAD

The tastes of the tropics are brought together in this tasty noodle salad, ideally served as a lunch or a light suppertime dish.

INGREDIENTS

Serves 4

10oz dried udon noodles
½ pineapple, peeled, cored and sliced
   into 1½ in rings
3 tbsp light brown sugar
4 tbsp fresh lime juice
4 tbsp coconut milk
2 tbsp fish sauce
2 tbsp grated fresh ginger
2 garlic cloves, finely chopped
1 ripe mango or 2 peaches, finely diced
black pepper
2 scallions, finely sliced, 2 red chilies,
   seeded and finely shredded, plus mint
   leaves, to garnish

NUTRITION NOTES

Per portion:	
Energy	350Kcals/1487kJ
Fat	4.49g
Saturated fat	0.05g
Cholesterol	0
Fiber	3.13g

COOK'S TIP
Use 4–6 canned pineapple rings in fruit juice, if fresh pineapple is not available. If you can't find Japanese udon noodles, substitute fettuccini or linguini. Choose ripe mangoes that have a smooth, unblemished skin and give slightly when you squeeze them gently.

1 Cook the noodles in a large saucepan of boiling water until tender, following the directions on the package. Drain, then refresh under cold water and drain again.

3 Mix the lime juice, coconut milk and fish sauce in a salad bowl. Add the remaining brown sugar, with the ginger and garlic, and whisk well. Add the noodles and pineapple.

2 Place the pineapple rings in a flameproof dish, sprinkle with about 2 tablespoons of the sugar and broil for about 5 minutes, or until golden. Cool slightly and cut into small dice.

4 Add the mango or peaches to the bowl and toss well. Sprinkle with the scallions, chilies and mint leaves before serving.

SPAGHETTI BOLOGNESE

INGREDIENTS

Serves 8

1 onion, chopped
2–3 garlic cloves, crushed
1¼ cups beef or
  chicken stock
1 lb extra-lean ground turkey
  or beef
1 28oz can chopped tomatoes
1 tsp dried basil
1 tsp dried oregano
4 tbsp tomato paste
1 lb button mushrooms, quartered
  and sliced
⅔ cup red wine
1 lb spaghetti
salt and black pepper

NUTRITION NOTES

Per portion:

Energy	321Kcals/1350kJ
Fat	4.1g
Saturated fat	1.3g
Cholesterol	33mg
Fiber	2.7g

1 Put the chopped onion and garlic into a nonstick saucepan with half the stock. Bring to a boil and cook for 5 minutes, until the onion is tender and the stock has reduced completely.

COOK'S TIP
Sautéing vegetables in fat-free stock rather than oil is an easy way of saving calories and fat. Choose fat-free stock to reduce even more.

2 Add the turkey or beef and cook for 5 minutes, breaking up the meat with a fork. Add the tomatoes, herbs and tomato paste, bring to a boil, then cover and simmer for 1 hour.

3 Meanwhile, cook the mushrooms in a nonstick saucepan with the wine for 5 minutes or until the wine has evaporated. Add the mushrooms to the meat with salt and pepper to taste.

4 Cook the pasta in a large pan of boiling salted water for 8–12 minutes, until tender. Drain thoroughly. Serve topped with the meat sauce.

BAKED RATATOUILLE WITH PENNE

INGREDIENTS

Serves 6

1 small eggplant
2 zucchini, thickly sliced
7oz firm tofu, cubed
3 tablespoons dark soy sauce
1 garlic clove, crushed
2 tsp sesame seeds
1 red bell pepper, seeded and sliced
1 onion, finely chopped
1–2 garlic cloves, crushed
⅔ cup vegetable stock
3 firm ripe tomatoes, skinned, seeded
   and quartered
1 tbsp chopped mixed herbs
8oz penne or other pasta shapes
salt and black pepper
crusty bread, to serve

1 Wash the eggplant and cut into 1in cubes. Put into a colander with the zucchini, sprinkle with salt and allow to drain for 30 minutes.

2 Mix the tofu with the soy sauce, garlic and sesame seeds. Cover and marinate for 30 minutes.

3 Put the pepper, onion and garlic into a saucepan with the stock. Bring to a boil, cover and cook for 5 minutes until tender. Remove the lid and boil until all the stock has evaporated. Add the tomatoes and herbs to the pan and cook for another 3 minutes, then add the rinsed eggplant and zucchini and cook until tender. Season to taste.

COOK'S TIP
Tofu is a low-fat protein, but it is very bland. Marinating adds plenty of flavor – make sure you leave it for the full 30 minutes.

4 Meanwhile, cook the pasta in a large pot of boiling, salted water according to the package instructions, until *al dente*, then drain thoroughly. Preheat the broiler. Toss the pasta with the vegetables and tofu. Transfer to a shallow ovenproof dish and broil until lightly toasted. Serve with bread.

NUTRITION NOTES	
Per portion:	
Energy	208Kcals/873kJ
Fat	3.7g
Saturated fat	0.5g
Cholesterol	0
Fiber	3.9g

Sweet and Sour Peppers with Pasta

A tasty and colorful low
fat dish – perfect for lunch
or supper.

INGREDIENTS

Serves 4
1 red, 1 yellow and 1 orange bell pepper
1 garlic clove, crushed
2 tbsp capers
2 tbsp raisins
1 tsp whole-grain mustard
rind and juice of 1 lime
1 tsp honey
2 tbsp chopped cilantro
8oz pasta bows
salt and black pepper
shavings of Parmesan cheese, to serve
   (optional)

1 Quarter the peppers and remove the stalks and seeds. Put the quarters into boiling water and cook for 10–15 minutes, until tender. Drain and rinse under cold water, then peel off the skin and cut the flesh into strips lengthwise.

2 Put the garlic, capers, raisins, mustard, lime rind and juice, honey, cilantro and seasoning into a bowl and whisk together.

3 Cook the pasta in a large pot of boiling, salted water for 10–12 minutes, until *al dente*. Drain thoroughly.

4 Return the pasta to the pot and add the pepper strips and dressing. Heat gently, tossing to mix. Transfer to a warm serving bowl and serve with a few shavings of Parmesan cheese, if using.

NUTRITION NOTES	
Per portion:	
Energy	268Kcals/1125kJ
Fat	2.0g
Saturated fat	0.5g
Cholesterol	1.3mg
Fiber	4.3g

PASTA WITH CHICKPEA SAUCE

This is a delicious, and very speedy, low fat dish. The quality of canned beans and tomatoes is so good that it is possible to transform them into a very fresh-tasting pasta sauce in minutes. Choose whatever pasta shapes you like, although hollow shapes, such as penne (quills) or shells are particularly good with this sauce.

INGREDIENTS

Serves 6

1 lb penne or other pasta shapes
2 tsp olive oil
1 onion, thinly sliced
1 red bell pepper, seeded and sliced
1 14oz can chopped tomatoes
1 15oz can chickpeas
2 tbsp dry vermouth (optional)
1 tsp dried oregano
1 large bay leaf
2 tbsp capers
salt and black pepper
fresh oregano, to garnish

COOK'S TIP
Choose fresh or dried unfilled pasta for this dish. Whichever you choose, cook it in a large pot of water so that the pasta keeps separate and doesn't stick together. Fresh pasta takes 2–4 minutes to cook and dried pasta 8–10 minutes. Cook pasta until it is *al dente* – firm and neither too hard nor too soft.

NUTRITION NOTES

Per portion:

Energy	268Kcals/1125kJ
Fat	2.0g
Saturated fat	0.5g
Cholesterol	1.3mg
Fiber	4.3g

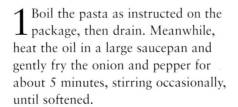

1 Boil the pasta as instructed on the package, then drain. Meanwhile, heat the oil in a large saucepan and gently fry the onion and pepper for about 5 minutes, stirring occasionally, until softened.

2 Add the tomatoes, chickpeas with their liquid, vermouth (if desired), herbs and capers and stir well.

3 Season to taste and bring to a boil, then simmer for about 10 minutes. Remove the bay leaf and mix in the pasta. Reheat and serve hot, garnished with sprigs of oregano.

PAPPARDELLE AND PROVENÇAL SAUCE

INGREDIENTS

Serves 4

2 small red onions
⅔ cup vegetable stock
1–2 garlic cloves, crushed
4 tbsp red wine
2 zucchini, cut in fingers
1 yellow bell pepper, seeded and sliced
1 14oz can tomatoes
2 tsp fresh thyme
1 tsp sugar
12oz pappardelle or other
  ribbon pasta
salt and black pepper
fresh thyme and 6 black olives, pitted
  and coarsely chopped, to garnish

NUTRITION NOTES

Per portion:
Energy	369Kcals/1550kJ
Fat	2.5g
Saturated fat	0.4g
Cholesterol	0
Fiber	4.3g

1 Cut each onion into eight wedges through the root end, to hold them together during cooking. Put into a saucepan with the stock and garlic. Bring to a boil, cover and simmer for 5 minutes, until tender.

2 Add the red wine, zucchini, yellow pepper, tomatoes, thyme, sugar and seasoning. Bring to a boil and cook gently for 5–7 minutes, shaking the pan occasionally to coat the vegetables with the sauce. (Do not overcook the vegetables. They are much nicer if they remain slightly crunchy.)

3 Cook the pasta in a large pot of boiling, salted water according to the package instructions, until *al dente*. Drain thoroughly.

4 Transfer the pasta to warmed serving plates and top with the vegetables. Garnish with fresh thyme and chopped black olives.

BASIC PASTA DOUGH
To make fresh pasta, sift 1¾ cups all-purpose flour and a pinch of salt onto a work surface and make a well in the center. Break two eggs into the well, and add 2 tsp cold water. Using a fork, beat the eggs gently, then gradually draw in the flour from the sides to make a thick paste. When the mixture becomes too stiff to use a fork, use your hands to mix to a firm dough. Knead for 5 minutes, until smooth. Wrap in plastic wrap and allow to rest for 20–30 minutes before rolling out and cutting.

SPAGHETTI ALLA CARBONARA

This is a variation on the classic charcoal-burner's spaghetti, using turkey bacon and low fat cream cheese instead of the traditional bacon and egg.

INGREDIENTS

Serves 4

5oz smoked turkey bacon
oil, for frying
1 medium onion, chopped
1–2 garlic cloves, crushed
⅔ cup chicken stock
⅔ cup dry white wine
7oz low fat cream cheese
1 lb chili and garlic-flavored spaghetti
2 tbsp chopped fresh parsley
salt and black pepper
shavings of Parmesan cheese,
    to serve

1 Cut the turkey bacon into ½in strips. Fry quickly in a nonstick pan for 2–3 minutes. Add the onion, garlic and stock to the pan. Bring to a boil, cover and simmer for about 5 minutes, until tender.

COOK'S TIP
If you can't find chili and garlic-flavored spaghetti, use plain spaghetti and add a small amount of fresh chili and garlic in step 4 or use the pasta of your choice.

2 Add the wine and boil rapidly until reduced by half. Whisk in the cream cheese and season to taste.

3 Meanwhile, cook the spaghetti in a large pot of boiling, salted water for 10–12 minutes, until *al dente*. Drain thoroughly.

4 Return the spaghetti to the pan with the sauce and parsley, toss well and serve immediately with a few thin shavings of Parmesan cheese.

NUTRITION NOTES

Per portion:

Energy	500Kcals/2102kJ
Fat	3.3g
Saturated fat	0.5g
Cholesterol	21mg
Fiber	4g

Fruit, Ham and French Bread Pizza

French bread makes a great pizza base. For a really speedy recipe, use ready-made pizza topping instead of the tomato sauce and cook the pizzas under a hot broiler for a few minutes to melt the cheese, instead of baking them in the oven.

INGREDIENTS

Serves 4

2 small baguettes

1¼ cups tomato sauce

3oz lean sliced cooked ham

4 canned pineapple rings, drained and chopped

½ small green bell pepper, seeded and cut into thin strips

2oz reduced fat aged Cheddar cheese

salt and black pepper

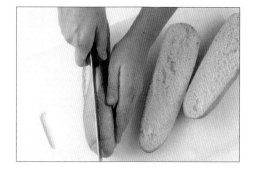

1 Preheat the oven to 400F°. Cut the baguettes in half lengthwise and toast the cut sides until crisp and golden.

> **Cook's Tip**
> If you prefer, omit the ham and substitute cooked chicken, peeled shrimp or tuna.

2 Spread the tomato sauce over the toasted baguettes.

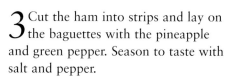

3 Cut the ham into strips and lay on the baguettes with the pineapple and green pepper. Season to taste with salt and pepper.

4 Grate the cheese and sprinkle on top. Bake for 15–20 minutes, until crisp and golden.

NUTRITION NOTES	
Per portion:	
Energy	111Kcals/468.7kJ
Fat	3.31g
Saturated fat	1.63g
Cholesterol	18.25mg
Fiber	0.79g

BULGUR AND MINT SALAD

Serves 4

1⅔ cups bulgur
4 tomatoes
4 small zucchini, thinly sliced
   lengthwise
4 scallions, sliced on the diagonal
8 dried apricots, chopped
¼ cup raisins
juice of 1 lemon
2 tbsp tomato juice
3 tbsp chopped fresh mint
1 garlic clove, crushed
salt and black pepper
sprig of fresh mint, to garnish

1 Put the bulgur into a large bowl. Add enough boiling water to come 1in above the level of the wheat. Allow to soak for 30 minutes, then drain well and squeeze out any excess water in a clean dishtowel.

2 Meanwhile, plunge the tomatoes into boiling water for 1 minute and then into cold water. Slip off the skins. Halve, remove the seeds and cores and coarsely chop the flesh.

3 Stir the chopped tomatoes, zucchini, scallions, apricots and raisins into the bulgur.

NUTRITION NOTES	
Per portion:	
Energy	293Kcals/1231kJ
Fat	1.69g
Saturated fat	0.28g
Fiber	2.25g

4 Put the lemon and tomato juice, mint, garlic clove and seasoning into a small bowl and whisk together with a fork. Pour onto the salad and mix well. Chill for at least 1 hour. Serve garnished with a sprig of mint.

CHILI BEAN BAKE

The contrasting textures of sauce, beans, vegetables and a crunchy cornbread topping make this a memorable meal.

INGREDIENTS

Serves 4
1¼ cups red kidney beans
1 bay leaf
1 large onion, finely chopped
1 garlic clove, crushed
2 celery stalks, sliced
1 tsp ground cumin
1 tsp chili powder
1 14oz can chopped tomatoes
1 tbsp tomato paste
1 tsp dried mixed herbs
1 tbsp lemon juice
1 yellow bell pepper, seeded and diced
salt and black pepper
mixed salad, to serve

For the cornbread topping
1½ cups cornmeal
1 tbsp whole-wheat flour
1 tsp baking powder
1 egg, beaten
¾ cup skim milk

1 Soak the beans overnight in cold water. Drain and rinse well. Pour 4 cups water into a large, heavy saucepan, add the beans and bay leaf and boil rapidly for 10 minutes. Lower the heat, cover and simmer for 35–40 minutes or until the beans are tender.

2 Add the onion, garlic, celery, cumin, chili powder, chopped tomatoes, tomato paste and dried mixed herbs. Half cover the pan with a lid and simmer for another 10 minutes.

NUTRITION NOTES	
Per portion:	
Energy	399Kcals/1675kJ
Protein	22.86g
Fat	4.65g
Saturated fat	0.86g
Fiber	11.59g

3 Stir in the lemon juice, yellow pepper and seasoning. Simmer for another 8–10 minutes, stirring occasionally, until the vegetables are just tender. Discard the bay leaf and spoon the mixture into a large casserole.

4 Preheat the oven to 425°F. To make the topping, put the cornmeal, flour, baking powder and a pinch of salt into a bowl and mix together. Make a well in the center and add the egg and milk. Mix and pour over the bean mixture. Bake for 20 minutes or until brown. Serve hot with mixed salad.

SPICY BEAN HOT POT

INGREDIENTS

Serves 4

3 cups button mushrooms
1 tbsp sunflower oil
2 onions, sliced
1 garlic clove, crushed
1 tbsp red wine vinegar
1 14oz can chopped tomatoes
1 tbsp tomato paste
1 tbsp Worcestershire sauce
1 tbsp whole-grain mustard
1 tbsp dark brown sugar
1 cup vegetable stock
1 14oz can red kidney beans,
    drained
1 14oz can cannellini beans,
    drained
1 bay leaf
½ cup raisins
salt and black pepper
chopped fresh parsley, to garnish

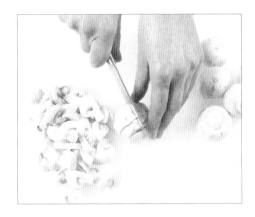

1 Wipe the mushrooms, then cut them into small pieces. Set aside.

2 Heat the oil in a large saucepan or flameproof casserole, add the onions and garlic and cook over low heat for 10 minutes until soft.

3 Add all the remaining ingredients except the mushrooms and seasoning. Bring to a boil, lower the heat and simmer for 10 minutes.

4 Add the mushrooms and simmer for 5 more minutes. Stir in salt and pepper to taste. Transfer to warm plates and sprinkle with parsley.

NUTRITION NOTES	
Per portion:	
Energy	280Kcals/1175kJ
Fat	4.5g
Saturated fat	0.5g
Cholesterol	0

BEAN PASTE WITH BROILED ENDIVE

The slightly bitter flavors of the radicchio and endive make a wonderful marriage with the creamy bean paste. Walnut oil adds a nutty taste, but olive oil could also be used.

INGREDIENTS

Serves 4
1 14oz can cannellini beans
3 tbsp low fat ricotta cheese
finely grated rind and juice of
   1 large orange
1 tbsp finely chopped
   fresh rosemary
4 Belgian endives
2 medium heads radicchio
2 tbsp walnut oil
shreds of orange rind, to garnish
   (optional)

1 Drain the beans, rinse, and drain again. Pulse the beans in a blender or food processor with the ricotta cheese, orange rind, orange juice and rosemary. Set aside.

2 Cut the heads of endive in half lengthwise.

3 Cut each radicchio head into eight wedges. Preheat the broiler.

4 Lay out the endive and radicchio on a baking tray and brush with the walnut oil. Broil for 2–3 minutes. Serve with the bean paste and sprinkle with the orange shreds, if using.

NUTRITION NOTES	
Per portion:	
Energy	103Kcals/432kJ
Protein	6.22g
Fat	1.54g
Saturated fat	0.4g
Fiber	6.73g

LENTIL BOLOGNESE

A really useful sauce to serve with pasta, as a pancake stuffing or even as a protein-packed sauce for vegetables.

INGREDIENTS

Serves 6

3 tbsp olive oil
1 onion, chopped
2 garlic cloves, crushed
2 carrots, coarsely grated
2 celery stalks, chopped
⅔ cup red lentils
1 14oz can chopped tomatoes
2 tbsp tomato paste
2 cups stock
1 tbsp fresh marjoram, chopped, or
  1 tsp dried marjoram
salt and black pepper

1 Heat the oil in a large saucepan and gently fry the onion, garlic, carrots and celery for about 5 minutes, until they are soft.

NUTRITION NOTES	
Per portion:	
Energy	103Kcals/432kJ
Fat	2.19g
Saturated fat	0.85g
Fiber	2.15g

2 Add the lentils, tomatoes, tomato paste, stock, marjoram and seasoning to the pan.

3 Bring the mixture to a boil, then partially cover with a lid and simmer for 20 minutes, until thick and soft. Use the sauce as required.

COOK'S TIP
You can easily reduce the fat in this recipe by using less olive oil, or substituting a little of the stock and cooking the vegetables over low heat in a non-stick frying pan until they are soft.

Vegetable Biryani

This exotic dish made from everyday ingredients will be appreciated by vegetarians and meat-eaters alike. It is extremely low in fat, but packed full of exciting flavors.

Ingredients

Serves 4–6
1 cup long-grain rice
2 whole cloves
seeds of 2 cardamom pods
2 cups vegetable stock
2 garlic cloves
1 small onion, coarsely chopped
1 tsp cumin seeds
1 tsp ground coriander
½ tsp ground turmeric
½ tsp chili powder
1 large potato, peeled and cut into
    1in cubes
2 carrots, sliced
½ cauliflower, broken into florets
2oz green beans, cut into
    1in lengths
2 tbsp chopped cilantro
2 tbsp lime juice
salt and black pepper
sprig of cilantro, to garnish

Nutrition Notes

Per portion:
Energy	175Kcals/737kJ
Protein	3.66g
Fat	0.78g
Saturated fat	0.12g
Fiber	0.58g

Cook's Tip
Substitute other vegetables, if you like. Zucchini, broccoli, parsnip and sweet potatoes would all be excellent choices.

1 Put the rice, cloves and cardamom seeds into a large, heavy saucepan. Pour in the stock and bring to a boil.

2 Reduce the heat, cover and simmer for 20 minutes, or until all the stock has been absorbed.

3 Meanwhile put the garlic cloves, onion, cumin seeds, coriander, ground turmeric, chili powder and seasoning into a blender or coffee grinder with 2 tablespoons water. Blend to a smooth paste.

4 Preheat the oven to 350°F. Spoon the spicy paste into a large flameproof casserole and cook over low heat for about 2 minutes, stirring occasionally.

5 Add the potato, carrots, cauliflower florets, beans and 6 tbsp water. Cover and cook over low heat for 12 more minutes, stirring occasionally. Add the chopped cilantro.

6 Remove the cloves and spoon the rice over the vegetables. Sprinkle with the lime juice. Cover and cook in the oven for 25 minutes, or until the vegetables are tender. Fluff up the rice with a fork before serving and garnish with a sprig of fresh cilantro.

COCONUT RICE

A delicious alternative to plain boiled rice. Brown or white rice will both work well.

INGREDIENTS

Serves 6

2 cups long-grain rice
1 cup water
2 cups coconut milk
½ tsp salt
2 tbsp sugar
fresh shredded coconut, to garnish

1 Wash the rice in cold water until it runs clear. Place water, coconut milk, salt and sugar in a heavy saucepan or flameproof casserole.

COOK'S TIP
Coconut milk is available in cans, but if you cannot find it, use creamed coconut mixed with water according to the package instructions.

2 Add the rice, cover and bring to a boil. Reduce the heat to low and simmer for 15–20 minutes or until the rice is tender to the bite and cooked through.

3 Turn off the heat and allow the rice to rest in the saucepan for another 5–10 minutes.

4 Fluff up the rice with chopsticks or a fork before serving garnished with shredded coconut.

NUTRITION NOTES

Per portion:
Energy	322.5Kcals/1371kJ
Fat	2.49g
Saturated fat	1.45g
Cholesterol	0
Fiber	0.68g

JASMINE RICE

Perfectly cooked rice makes an ideal, low fat accompaniment to many low fat dishes such as vegetable chili and vegetable Bolognese.

INGREDIENTS

Serves 6

2 cups long-grain rice
½ tsp salt

NUTRITION NOTES

Per portion:
Energy	270.8Kcals/1152kJ
Fat	0.75g
Saturated fat	0
Cholesterol	0
Fiber	0.37g

COOK'S TIP
An electric rice cooker both cooks the rice and keeps it warm. Different sizes and models are available. The top of the line is a nonstick version which is expensive but well worth the money if you eat rice a lot.

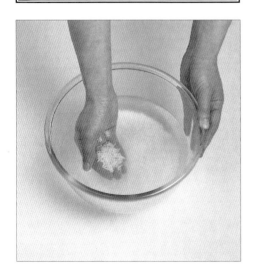

1 Rinse the rice in several changes of cold water until the water stays clear.

2 Put the rice in a heavy saucepan or flameproof casserole and add 3 cups cold water and salt. Bring the rice to a vigorous boil, uncovered, over high heat.

3 Stir and reduce the heat to low. Cover and simmer for up to 20 minutes, or until all the water has been absorbed. Remove from the heat and allow to stand for 10 minutes.

4 Remove the lid and stir the rice gently with chopsticks or a fork to fluff up and separate the grains.

MEAT AND POULTRY

Make the most of the wide range of leaner cuts of meat available to make delicious, low fat dishes. Included here are tempting, light and nutritious main courses, which are packed with flavor, try spicy Thai Beef Salad or Tandoori Chicken Kebabs for an *al fresco* summer lunch, Ragoût of Veal, Chicken, Carrot and Leek Packages or Venison with Cranberry Sauce for a special occasion dinner. If you are feeding a family, there are plenty of recipes here that will please, from Turkey and Tomato Hot Pot to Barbecued Chicken.

THAI BEEF SALAD

A hearty salad of beef, laced with a chili and lime dressing.

INGREDIENTS

Serves 6

6 lean sirloin steaks, 3oz each
1 red onion, finely sliced
$^1/_2$ cucumber, finely sliced
   into matchsticks
1 lemongrass stalk, finely chopped
2 tbsp chopped scallions
juice of 2 limes
1–2 tbsp fish sauce
2–4 red chilies, finely sliced, to garnish
cilantro, Chinese mustard cress and
   mint leaves, to garnish

NUTRITION NOTES	
Per portion:	
Energy	101Kcals/424kJ
Fat	3.8g
Saturated fat	1.7g
Cholesterol	33.4mg
Fiber	0.28g

COOK'S TIP
Round or tenderloin steaks would work just as well in this recipe. Choose good-quality lean steaks and remove and discard any visible fat.

1 Broil the sirloin steaks until they are medium-rare, then allow to rest for 10–15 minutes.

2 When cool, thinly slice the beef and put the slices in a large bowl.

3 Add the sliced onion, cucumber matchsticks and lemongrass.

4 Add the scallions. Toss and season with lime juice and fish sauce. Serve at room temperature or chilled, garnished with the chilies, cilantro, mustard cress and mint.

RAGOÛT OF VEAL

If you are looking for a low-calorie dish to treat yourself – or some guests – then this is perfect, and quick, too.

INGREDIENTS

Serves 4

12oz veal cutlets or loin
2 tsp olive oil
10–12 tiny onions, kept whole
1 yellow bell pepper, seeded and
cut into eighths
1 orange or red bell pepper, seeded
and cut into eighths
3 tomatoes, peeled
and quartered
4 fresh basil sprigs
2 tbsp dry vermouth or sherry
salt and black pepper

NUTRITION NOTES

Per portion:
Energy	158Kcals/665.5kJ
Fat	4.97g
Saturated Fat	1.14g
Cholesterol	63mg
Fiber	2.5g

1 Trim off any fat and cut the veal into cubes. Heat the oil in a frying pan and gently stir-fry the veal and onions until browned.

2 After a couple of minutes, add the peppers and tomatoes. Continue stir-frying for another 4–5 minutes.

COOK'S TIP
Lean beef or pork fillet may be used instead of veal, if you prefer. Shallots can replace the onions.

3 Add half the basil leaves, coarsely chopped (keep some for garnish), the vermouth or sherry, and seasoning. Cook, stirring frequently, for another 10 minutes, or until the meat is tender.

4 Sprinkle with the remaining basil leaves and serve hot.

VENISON WITH CRANBERRY SAUCE

Venison steaks are now widely available. Lean and low in fat, they make a healthy choice for a special occasion. Served with a sauce of fresh seasonal cranberries, port and ginger, they make a dish with a wonderful combination of flavors.

INGREDIENTS

Serves 4

1 orange
1 lemon
1 cup fresh or frozen
  cranberries
1 tsp grated fresh ginger
1 thyme sprig, plus extra to garnish
1 tsp Dijon mustard
4 tbsp red currant jelly
⅔ cup ruby port
2 tsp sunflower oil
4 venison steaks, 3½oz each
2 shallots, finely chopped
salt and black pepper
mashed potato and broccoli, to serve

NUTRITION NOTES

Per portion:
Energy	250Kcals/1055.5kJ
Fat	4.39g
Saturated fat	1.13g
Cholesterol	50mg
Fiber	1.59g

COOK'S TIP
When frying venison, always remember: the briefer the better. Venison will turn to leather if subjected to fierce heat after it has reached the medium-rare stage. If you dislike any hint of pink, cook it to this stage, then let it rest in a low oven for a few minutes.

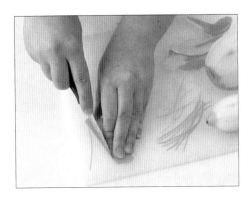

1 Pare the rind from half the orange and half the lemon using a vegetable peeler, then cut into very fine strips.

2 Blanch the strips in a small pan of boiling water for about 5 minutes, until tender. Drain the strips and refresh under cold water.

3 Squeeze the juice from the orange and lemon, then pour into a small pan. Add the cranberries, ginger, thyme sprig, mustard, red currant jelly and port. Cook over low heat until the jelly melts.

4 Bring the sauce to a boil, stirring occasionally, then cover the pan and reduce the heat. Cook gently for about 15 minutes, until the cranberries are just tender.

VARIATION
Substitute red currants for the cranberries. Stir them into the sauce toward the end of cooking with the orange and lemon rinds.

5 Heat the oil in a heavy frying pan, add the venison and cook over high heat for 2–3 minutes.

6 Turn over the steaks and add the shallots to the pan. Cook the steaks on the other side for 2–3 minutes, depending on whether you like rare or medium-cooked meat.

7 Just before the end of cooking, pour in the sauce and add the strips of orange and lemon rind.

8 Allow the sauce to bubble for a few seconds to thicken slightly, then remove the thyme sprig and adjust the seasoning to taste.

9 Transfer the venison steaks to warmed plates and spoon the sauce over them. Garnish with thyme sprigs and serve accompanied by mashed potato and broccoli.

BARBECUED CHICKEN

INGREDIENTS

Serves 4 or 8

8 small chicken pieces
2 limes, cut into wedges, 2 red chilies,
*   finely sliced, and 2 lemongrass stalks,*
*   to garnish*
rice, to serve

For the marinade
2 lemongrass stalks, chopped
1in piece fresh ginger
6 garlic cloves
4 shallots
¹/₂ bunch cilantro
1 tbsp sugar
¹/₂ cup coconut milk
2 tbsp fish sauce
2 tbsp soy sauce

COOK'S TIP
Don't eat the skin of the chicken –
it's only left on to keep the flesh
moist during cooking. Coconut
milk makes a good base for a
marinade or sauce, as it is low in
calories and fat.

NUTRITION NOTES

Per portion (for 8):

Energy	106Kcals/449kJ
Fat	2.05g
Saturated fat	1.10g
Cholesterol	1.10mg
Fiber	109g

1 To make the marinade, put all the
ingredients into a food processor
and process until smooth.

2 Put the chicken pieces in a dish
and add the marinade. Set aside in a
cool place to marinate for at least
4 hours or overnight.

3 Preheat the oven to 400°F. Put
the chicken pieces on a rack on a
baking tray. Brush the chicken with the
marinade and bake for 20–30 minutes,
or until the chicken is cooked and gold-
en brown. Turn the pieces over halfway
through cooking and brush with more
marinade.

4 Garnish with lime wedges, finely
sliced red chilies and lemongrass
stalks. Serve with rice.

TANDOORI CHICKEN SKEWERS

This dish originates from the plains of the Punjab, at the foot of the Himalayas, where food is traditionally cooked in clay ovens known as tandoors – hence the name.

INGREDIENTS

Serves 4
4 boneless, skinless chicken breasts,
   about 3¹/₂oz each
1 tbsp lemon juice
3 tbsp tandoori paste
3 tbsp low fat plain yogurt
1 garlic clove, crushed
2 tbsp chopped cilantro
1 small onion, cut into wedges and
   separated into layers
1 tsp oil, for brushing
salt and black pepper
cilantro sprigs, to garnish
rice pilaf and nan, to serve

1 Chop the chicken breasts into 1in cubes, put in a bowl and add the lemon juice, tandoori paste, yogurt, garlic, cilantro and seasoning. Cover and let marinate in the fridge for 2–3 hours.

2 Preheat the broiler to high. Thread alternate pieces of chicken and onion onto four skewers.

COOK'S TIP
Use chopped, boned and skinned chicken thighs, or strips of turkey breasts, for a cheaper and equally low fat alternative.

3 Brush onions with a little oil, lay the skewers on a broiler rack and cook for 10–12 minutes, turning once.

4 Garnish the kebabs with cilantro and serve at once with rice pilaf and nan.

NUTRITION NOTES

Per portion:
Energy	215.7Kcals/91.2kJ
Fat	4.2g
Saturated fat	0.27g
Cholesterol	122mg
Fiber	0.22g

CHICKEN, CARROT AND LEEK PACKAGES

These intriguing packages may sound a bit fussy for everyday eating, but actually they take very little time, and you can freeze them so they'll be ready to cook when needed.

INGREDIENTS

Serves 4

4 *chicken fillets or skinless, boneless breasts*
2 *small leeks, sliced*
2 *carrots, grated*
2 *pitted black olives, chopped*
1 *garlic clove, crushed*
4 *anchovy fillets, halved lengthwise*
salt and black pepper
black olives and herb sprigs, to garnish

1 Preheat the oven to 400°F. Season the chicken well.

2 Cut out four sheets of lightly greased parchment paper about 9in square. Divide the leeks equally among them. Put a piece of chicken on top of each.

3 Stir together the carrots, olives and garlic. Season lightly and place on top of the chicken portions. Top each with two of the anchovy fillets.

4 Carefully wrap up each package, making sure the paper folds are sealed. Bake for 20 minutes and serve hot, in the paper, garnished with black olives and herb sprigs.

NUTRITION NOTES

Per portion:

Energy	154Kcals/651kJ
Fat	2.37g
Saturated fat	0.45g
Cholesterol	78.75mg
Fiber	2.1g

COOK'S TIP
Skinless, boneless chicken is low in fat and is an excellent source of protein. Small, skinless turkey breast fillets also work well in this recipe and make a tasty change.

THAI CHICKEN AND VEGETABLE STIR-FRY

INGREDIENTS

Serves 4

1 piece lemongrass (or the rind of
   ½ lemon)
½in piece fresh ginger
1 large garlic clove
2 tbsp sunflower oil
10oz lean chicken
½ red bell pepper, seeded and sliced
½ green bell pepper, seeded and sliced
4 scallions, chopped
2 medium carrots, cut into matchsticks
4oz thin green beans
1oz peanuts, lightly crushed
2 tbsp oyster sauce
pinch of sugar
salt and black pepper
cilantro leaves, to garnish
steamed rice, to serve

NUTRITION NOTES

Per portion:	
Energy	106Kcals/449kJ
Fat	2.05g
Saturated fat	1.10g
Cholesterol	1.10mg
Fiber	109g

1 Thinly slice the lemongrass or lemon rind. Peel and chop the ginger and garlic. Heat the oil in a frying pan over high heat. Add the lemongrass or lemon rind, ginger and garlic, and stir-fry for 30 seconds, until brown.

2 Add the chicken and stir-fry for 2 minutes. Then add all the vegetables and stir-fry for 4–5 minutes, until the chicken is cooked and the vegetables are almost cooked.

3 Finally, stir in the peanuts, oyster sauce, sugar and seasoning to taste. Stir-fry for another minute to blend the flavors. Serve immediately, sprinkled with the cilantro leaves and accompanied by steamed rice.

COOK'S TIP
Make this quick supper dish a little hotter by adding more fresh ginger, if desired.

DUCK-BREAST SALAD

Tender slices of succulent cooked duck breasts served with a salad of mixed pasta, fruit and vegetables, tossed together in a light dressing, makes this a gourmet dish that will impress friends and family alike.

INGREDIENTS

Serves 6

2 small duck breasts, boned
1 tsp coriander, crushed
12oz rigatoni or penne pasta
⅔ cup fresh orange juice
1 tbsp lemon juice
2 tsp honey
1 shallot, finely chopped
1 garlic clove, crushed
1 celery stalk, chopped
3oz dried cherries
3 tbsp port
1 tbsp chopped fresh mint, plus extra to garnish
2 tbsp chopped cilantro, plus extra to garnish
1 eating apple, diced
2 oranges, segmented
salt and black pepper

COOK'S TIP
Choose skinless duck breasts to reduce both fat and calories. Crush your own whole spices, such as coriander seeds, to create fresh, aromatic, spicy flavors. Prepared ground spices lose their flavor more quickly than whole spices, which are best freshly ground just before use.

2 Cook the pasta in a large pot of boiling, salted water according to the package instructions, until *al dente*. Drain thoroughly and rinse under cold running water. Set aside to cool.

4 Slice the duck breasts very thinly. (They should be pink in the center.)

5 Put the pasta into a large bowl, then add the dressing, diced apple and segments of orange. Toss well to coat the pasta. Transfer the salad to a serving plate with the duck slices and garnish with the extra mint and cilantro.

NUTRITION NOTES

Per portion:
Energy	348Kcals/1460kJ
Fat	3.8g
Saturated fat	0.9g
Cholesterol	55mg
Fiber	3g

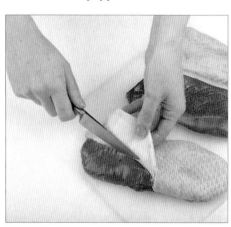

1 Remove the skin and fat from the duck breasts and season with salt and pepper. Rub with coriander seeds. Preheat the broiler, then broil the duck for 10 minutes on each side. Wrap in foil and let stand for 20 minutes.

3 To make the dressing, put the orange juice, lemon juice, honey, shallot, garlic, celery, cherries, port, mint and cilantro into a bowl, whisk together and allow to marinate for 30 minutes.

Fragrant Chicken Curry

In this dish, the mildly spiced sauce is thickened using lentils rather than the traditional onions fried in ghee.

Ingredients

Serves 4–6

½ cup red lentils
2 tbsp mild curry powder
2 tsp ground coriander
1 tsp cumin seeds
2 cups vegetable stock
8 chicken thighs, skinned
8oz fresh shredded spinach, or frozen, thawed and well drained
1 tbsp chopped cilantro
salt and black pepper
sprigs of cilantro, to garnish
white or brown basmati rice and broiled poppadums, to serve

1 Rinse the lentils under cold running water. Put in a large, heavy saucepan with the curry powder, ground coriander, cumin seeds and vegetable stock.

2 Bring to a boil, then lower the heat. Cover and simmer gently for about 10 minutes.

Nutrition Notes

Per portion:
Energy	152Kcals/640kJ
Fat	4.9g
Saturated fat	1.3g
Added Sugar	0
Fiber	2.6g

Cook's Tip

Lentils are an excellent source of fiber, and add color and texture.

3 Add the chicken and spinach. Replace the cover and simmer gently for another 40 minutes, or until the chicken has cooked.

4 Stir in the chopped cilantro and season to taste. Serve garnished with cilantro and accompanied by the rice and broiled poppadums.

TURKEY AND PASTA BAKE

INGREDIENTS

Serves 4

10oz ground turkey
5oz smoked turkey bacon, chopped
1–2 garlic cloves, crushed
1 onion, finely chopped
2 carrots, diced
2 tbsp tomato paste
1¼ cups chicken stock
8oz rigatoni or penne pasta
2 tbsp grated Parmesan cheese
salt and black pepper

1 Brown the ground turkey in a non-stick saucepan, breaking up any large pieces with a wooden spoon, until well browned all over.

3 Preheat the oven to 350°F. Cook the pasta in a large pot of boiling, salted water according to the package instructions, until *al dente*. Drain thoroughly and mix with the turkey sauce.

4 Transfer to a shallow ovenproof dish and sprinkle with grated Parmesan cheese. Bake for 20–30 minutes, until lightly browned on top.

2 Add the chopped turkey bacon, garlic, onion, carrots, paste, stock and seasoning. Bring to a boil, cover and simmer for 1 hour, until tender.

COOK'S TIP
Ground chicken or extra lean ground beef work just as well in this tasty recipe.

NUTRITION NOTES

Per portion:
Energy	391Kcals/1641kJ
Fat	4.9g
Saturated fat	2.2g
Cholesterol	60mg
Fiber	3.5g

Turkey and Tomato Hot Pot

Here, turkey is turned into tasty meatballs in a rich tomato sauce.

Ingredients

Serves 4

1 slice white bread, crusts removed
2 tbsp skim milk
1 garlic clove, crushed
$^1\!/_2$ tsp caraway seeds
8oz ground turkey
1 egg white
$1^1\!/_2$ cups chicken stock
1 14oz can tomatoes
1 tbsp tomato paste
$^1\!/_2$ cup quick-cooking rice
salt and black pepper
fresh basil, to garnish
carrot and zucchini ribbons, to serve

1 Cut the bread into small cubes and put into a mixing bowl. Sprinkle over the milk and allow to soak for 5 minutes.

2 Add the garlic clove, caraway seeds, turkey and seasoning to the bread. Stir well.

3 Whisk the egg white until stiff, then fold, half at a time, into the turkey mixture. Chill for 10 minutes.

4 While the turkey mixture is chilling, put the stock, tomatoes and tomato paste into a large saucepan and bring to a boil.

5 Add the rice, stir and cook briskly for about 5 minutes. Turn the heat down to a gentle simmer.

6 Meanwhile, shape the turkey mixture into 16 small balls. Carefully drop them into the tomato stock and simmer for another 8–10 minutes, or until both the turkey balls and rice are cooked. Garnish with basil, and serve with carrot and zucchini ribbons.

Cook's Tips

To make carrot and zucchini ribbons, cut the vegetables lengthwise into thin strips using a vegetable peeler, and blanch or steam until lightly cooked.

Lean ground turkey is low in fat and is a good source of protein. It makes an ideal base for this tasty low-fat supper dish. Use ground chicken in place of turkey for an appetizing alternative.

Nutrition Notes

Per portion:

Energy	190Kcals/798kJ
Protein	18.04g
Fat	1.88g
Saturated fat	0.24g
Fiber	10.4g

FISH AND SEAFOOD

The range of fresh fish available in our supermarkets
is impressive, and fish is always a good choice for a
healthy low fat diet. Most fish, particularly white fish, is low
in fat and is a good source of protein. Oily fish contains more
fat than white fish, but also has high levels of essential fatty
acids which are vital for good health. Fish is quick and easy to
prepare and cook and is ideal for serving with fresh seasonal
vegetables as part of a healthy low fat meal. Try Cajun-style
Cod, Herbed Fishcakes with Lemon Sauce, Mediterranean
Fish Fillets or Curried Shrimp in Coconut Milk – just some of
the delicious, low fat recipes included in this chapter.

Cajun-style Cod

This recipe works equally well with any firm-fleshed fish – choose low fat fish, such as haddock or monkfish.

Nutrition Notes

Per portion:

Energy	137Kcals/577kJ
Protein	28.42g
Fat	1.75g
Saturated fat	0.26g
Fiber	0.06g

Ingredients

Serves 4

4 cod steaks, about
  6oz each
2 tbsp low fat plain yogurt
1 tbsp lime or lemon juice
1 garlic clove, crushed
1 tsp ground cumin
1 tsp paprika
1 tsp mustard powder
½ tsp cayenne pepper
½ tsp dried thyme
½ tsp dried oregano
nonstick cooking spray
lemon slices, to garnish
new potatoes and a mixed green salad,
  to serve

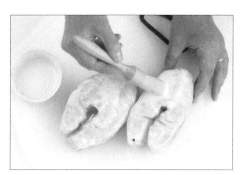

1 Pat the fish dry with paper towels. Combine the yogurt and lime or lemon juice and brush lightly over both sides of the fish.

2 Stir together the crushed garlic, spices and herbs. Coat both sides of the fish with the seasoning mix, rubbing in well.

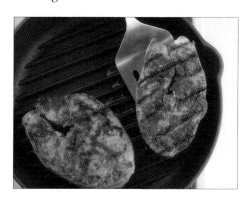

3 Spray a ridged broiler pan or heavy frying pan with nonstick cooking spray. Heat until very hot. Add the fish and cook over high heat for 4 minutes, or until the undersides are well browned.

4 Turn the steaks over and cook for another 4 minutes or until cooked through. Serve immediately, garnished with lemon and accompanied by new potatoes and a mixed salad.

FLOUNDER PROVENÇAL

Serves 4

4 large flounder fillets
2 small red onions
½ cup vegetable stock
4 tbsp dry red wine
1 garlic clove, crushed
2 zucchini, sliced
1 yellow bell pepper, seeded and sliced
1 14oz can chopped tomatoes
1 tbsp chopped fresh thyme
salt and black pepper
potato gratin, to serve

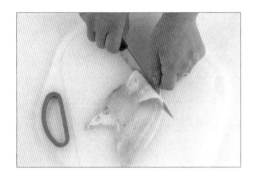

1 Preheat the oven to 350°F. If necessary, skin the fish: lay the flounder skin-side down and, holding the tail end, push a sharp knife between the skin and flesh in a sawing motion. Hold the knife at a slight angle with the blade towards the skin.

2 Cut each onion into eight wedges. Place in a heavy saucepan with the stock. Cover and simmer for 5 minutes. Uncover and continue to cook, stirring occasionally, until the stock has evaporated. Add the wine and garlic clove to the pan and continue to cook until the onions are soft.

3 Add the zucchini, yellow pepper, tomatoes and thyme and season to taste. Simmer for 3 minutes. Spoon the sauce into a large casserole.

COOK'S TIP
Skinless white fish fillets such as flounder or sand dab are low in fat and make an ideal tasty and nutritious basis for many low-fat recipes such as this one.

4 Fold each fillet in half and put on top of the sauce. Cover and cook in the oven for 15–20 minutes, until the fish is opaque and flakes easily. Serve with a potato gratin.

NUTRITION NOTES	
Per portion:	
Energy	191Kcals/802kJ
Protein	29.46g
Fat	3.77g
Saturated fat	0.61g
Fiber	1.97g

MONKFISH AND MUSSEL SKEWERS

Skinless white fish such as monkfish is a good source of protein while also being low in calories and fat. These attractive seafood kebabs, flavored with a light marinade, are excellent broiled or barbecued and served with herbed boiled rice and a mixed green salad.

INGREDIENTS

Serves 4

1 lb monkfish, skinned and boned
1 tsp olive oil
2 tbsp lemon juice
1 tsp paprika
1 garlic clove, crushed
4 turkey bacon strips
8 cooked mussels
8 raw shrimp
1 tbsp chopped fresh dill
salt and black pepper
lemon wedges, to garnish
salad leaves and long-grain and wild
*   rice, to serve*

1 Cut the monkfish into 1in cubes and place in a shallow glass dish. Combine the oil, lemon juice, paprika and garlic. Season with pepper.

2 Pour the marinade over the fish and toss to coat evenly. Cover and put in a cool place for 30 minutes.

3 Cut the turkey bacon strips in half and wrap each strip around a mussel. Thread onto skewers, alternating with the fish cubes and raw shrimps. Preheat the broiler to high.

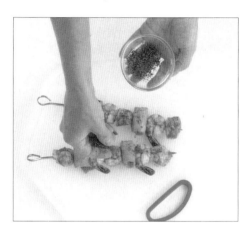

4 Broil the kebabs for 7–8 minutes, turning once and basting with the marinade. Sprinkle with chopped dill and salt. Garnish with lemon wedges and serve with salad and rice.

NUTRITION NOTES	
Per portion:	
Energy	133Kcals/560kJ
Protein	25.46g
Fat	3.23g
Saturated fat	0.77g
Fiber	0.12g

SOLE FILLETS BAKED IN A PAPER CASE

INGREDIENTS

Serves 4

4 sole or flounder fillets, about
  5 ounces each
½ small cucumber, sliced
4 lemon slices
4 tbsp dry white wine
sprigs of fresh dill, to garnish
potatoes and braised celery, to serve

For the yogurt hollandaise
½ cup low fat plain yogurt
1 tsp lemon juice
2 egg yolks
1 tsp Dijon mustard
salt and black pepper

1 Preheat the oven to 350°F. Cut out four heart shapes from nonstick parchment paper, each about 8 x 6 in.

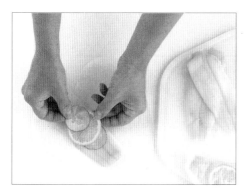

2 Place a sole fillet on one side of each paper heart. Arrange the cucumber and lemon slices on top of each fillet. Sprinkle with the wine and close the packages by turning the edges of the paper and twisting to secure. Put the packages on a baking sheet and cook for 15 minutes.

3 Meanwhile make the hollandaise. Beat together the yogurt, lemon juice and egg yolks in a double boiler or bowl placed over a saucepan. Cook over simmering water, stirring for about 15 minutes, or until thickened. (The sauce will become thinner after 10 minutes, but will thicken again.)

COOK'S TIP
Make sure that the paper packages are well sealed, so that none of the delicious juices can escape.

4 Remove from the heat and stir in the mustard. Season to taste with salt and pepper. Open the fish packages, garnish with a sprig of dill and serve accompanied with the sauce, new potatoes and braised celery.

NUTRITION NOTES

Per portion:

Energy	185Kcals/779kJ
Protein	29.27g
Fat	4.99g
Saturated fat	1.58g
Fiber	0.27g

HERBED FISHCAKES WITH LEMON SAUCE

The wonderful flavor of fresh herbs makes these fishcakes the catch of the day.

INGREDIENTS

Serves 4

12oz potatoes, coarsely chopped
5 tbsp skim milk
12oz haddock
*   fillets, skinned*
1 tbsp lemon juice
1 tbsp horseradish sauce
2 tbsp chopped fresh parsley
flour, for dusting
2 cups fresh whole-wheat bread crumbs
salt and black pepper
parsley sprigs, to garnish
sugar snap peas or snow peas and a
*   sliced tomato and onion salad,*
*   to serve*

For the lemon and chive sauce
thinly pared rind and juice of
*   ¹/₂ small lemon*
¹/₂ cup dry white wine
2 thin slices of fresh ginger
2 tsp cornstarch
2 tbsp chopped fresh chives

NUTRITION NOTES

Per portion:	
Energy	232Kcals/975kJ
Protein	19.99g
Fat	1.99g
Saturated fat	0.26g
Fiber	3.11g

COOK'S TIP
Dry white wine is a tasty fat-free basis for this herb sauce. Try using cider as an alternative to wine, for a change.

1 Cook the potatoes in a large saucepan of boiling water for 15–20 minutes. Drain and mash with the milk and season to taste.

2 Purée the fish together with the lemon juice and horseradish sauce in a blender or food processor. Mix with the potatoes and parsley.

3 With floured hands, shape the mixture into eight fishcakes and coat with the breadcrumbs. Chill in the fridge for 30 minutes.

4 Preheat the grill to medium and cook the fishcakes for 5 minutes on each side, until browned.

5 To make the sauce, cut the lemon rind into julienne strips and put into a large saucepan together with the lemon juice, wine and ginger. Season to taste with salt and pepper.

6 Simmer, uncovered, for about 6 minutes. Blend the cornstarch with 1 tbsp of cold water, add to the pan and simmer until clear. Stir in the chives immediately before serving.

7 Serve the sauce hot with the fishcakes, garnished with parsley sprigs and accompanied by peas and a tomato and onion salad.

STEAMED FISH WITH CHILI SAUCE

Steaming is one of the best – and lowest-fat – methods of cooking fish. By leaving the fish whole and on the bone, you'll find that all the delicious flavor and moistness is retained.

INGREDIENTS

Serves 6

1 large or 2 medium, firm fish like bass
    or grouper, scaled and cleaned
a fresh banana leaf or large piece
    of foil
2 tbsp rice wine
3 red chilies, seeded and finely sliced
2 garlic cloves, finely chopped
¾in piece of fresh ginger,
    finely shredded
2 lemongrass stalks, crushed and
    finely chopped
2 scallions, chopped
2 tbsp fish sauce
juice of 1 lime

For the chili sauce

10 red chilies, seeded and chopped
4 garlic cloves, chopped
4 tbsp fish sauce
1 tbsp sugar
5 tbsp lime juice

1 Rinse the fish under cold running water. Pat dry with paper towels. With a sharp knife, slash the skin of the fish a few times on both sides.

2 Place the fish on the banana leaf or foil. Combine the remaining ingredients and spread over the fish.

3 Place a small upturned plate in the bottom of a wok or large frying pan, and add about 2in boiling water. Lay the banana leaf or foil with the fish on top on the plate and cover with a lid. Steam for 10–15 minutes, or until the fish is cooked.

4 Meanwhile, put all the chili sauce ingredients in a food processor and process until smooth. You may need to add a little cold water to make the paste easier to process.

5 Serve the fish hot, on the banana leaf, if desired, with the sweet chili sauce to spoon over the top.

NUTRITION NOTES	
Per portion:	
Energy	170Kcals/721kJ
Fat	3.46g
Saturated fat	0.54g
Cholesterol	106mg
Fiber	0.35g

BAKED COD WITH TOMATOES

For the very best flavor, use firm sun-ripened tomatoes for the sauce and make sure it is fairly thick before spooning it over the cod.

INGREDIENTS

Serves 4
2 tsp olive oil
1 onion, chopped
2 garlic cloves, finely chopped
1 lb tomatoes, peeled, seeded and chopped
1 tsp tomato paste
4 tbsp dry white wine
4 tbsp chopped flat leaf parsley
4 cod steaks
2 tbsp dried bread crumbs
salt and black pepper
new potatoes and green salad, to serve

NUTRITION NOTES

Per portion:
Energy	151Kcals/647kJ
Fat	1.5g
Saturated fat	0.2g
Cholesterol	55.2mg
Fiber	2.42g

COOK'S TIP
For extra speed, use a 14oz can of chopped tomatoes in place of the fresh tomatoes and 1–2 tsp prepared minced garlic in place of the garlic cloves.

1 Preheat the oven to 375°F. Heat the oil in a pan and fry the onion for about 5 minutes. Add the garlic, tomatoes, tomato paste, wine and seasoning.

2 Bring the sauce just to a boil, then reduce the heat slightly and cook, uncovered, for 15–20 minutes, until thick. Stir in the parsley.

3 Grease an ovenproof dish, put in the cod cutlets and spoon an equal amount of the tomato sauce onto each. Sprinkle the dried bread crumbs over the top.

4 Bake for 20–30 minutes, basting the fish occasionally with the sauce, until the fish is tender and cooked through, and the bread crumbs are golden and crisp. Serve hot with new potatoes and a green salad.

MEDITERRANEAN FISH FILLETS

These low fat fish fillets are nicely complemented by boiled potatoes, broccoli and carrots.

INGREDIENTS

Serves 4

4 *white fish fillets, about*
  5oz each
⅓ *cup fish stock or dry white wine (or*
  a mixture of the two), for poaching
1 *bay leaf, a few black peppercorns*
  and a strip of pared lemon rind, for
  flavoring
chopped fresh parsley, to garnish

For the tomato sauce

1 *14oz can chopped tomatoes*
1 *garlic clove, crushed*
1 *tbsp pastis or other anise-*
  flavored liqueur
1 *tbsp drained capers*
12–16 *pitted black olives*
salt and black pepper

1 To make the sauce, place the chopped tomatoes, garlic, pastis, capers and olives in a saucepan. Season to taste with salt and pepper and cook over low heat for about 15 minutes, stirring occasionally.

2 Place the fish in a frying pan, pour over the stock and/or wine and add the bay leaf, peppercorns and lemon rind. Cover and simmer for 10 minutes or until it flakes easily.

3 Using a slotted spoon, transfer the fish into a heated dish. Strain the stock into the tomato sauce and boil to reduce slightly. Season the sauce, pour it over the fish and serve immediately, sprinkled with the chopped parsley.

COOK'S TIP
Remove skin from cutlets and reduce the quantity of olives to reduce calories and fat. Use 1 lb fresh tomatoes, skinned and chopped, in place of the canned tomatoes.

NUTRITION NOTES	
Per portion:	
Energy	165Kcals/685kJ
Fat	3.55g
Saturated fat	0.5g
Cholesterol	69mg

BAKED FISH IN BANANA LEAVES

Fish that is prepared in this way is particularly succulent and full of flavor. Fillets are used here, rather than whole fish, which is easier for those who don't like to mess with bones. It is a great dish for a barbecue.

INGREDIENTS

Serves 4

1 cup coconut milk
2 tbsp red curry paste
3 tbsp fish sauce
2 tbsp sugar
5 kafir lime leaves, torn
6oz fish fillets, such
  as snapper
6oz mixed vegetables, such as
  carrots or leeks, finely shredded
4 banana leaves or pieces of foil
2 tbsp shredded scallions,
  to garnish
2 red chilies, finely sliced, to garnish

NUTRITION NOTES

Per portion:
Energy	258Kcals/1094kJ
Fat	4.31g
Saturated fat	0.7g
Cholesterol	64.75mg
Fiber	1.23g

COOK'S TIP
Coconut milk is low in calories and fat and so makes an ideal basis for a low fat marinade or sauce. Choose colorful vegetables such as carrots, leeks and red bell pepper, to make the dish more attractive and appealing.

1 Combine the coconut milk, curry paste, fish sauce, sugar and kafir lime leaves in a shallow dish.

2 Marinate the fish in this mixture for 15–30 minutes. Preheat the oven to 400°F.

3 Lay a portion of the mixed vegetables on top of a banana leaf or piece of foil. Place a piece of fish on top with a little of its marinade.

4 Wrap the fish up by turning in the sides and ends of the leaf and secure with toothpicks. (With foil, just pinch the edges together.) Repeat with the rest of the fish.

5 Bake for 20–25 minutes or until the fish is cooked. Alternatively, cook under the broiler or on a barbecue. Just before serving, garnish the fish with a sprinkling of scallions and sliced red chilies.

PINEAPPLE CURRY WITH SEAFOOD

The delicate sweet and sour flavor of this curry comes from the pineapple, and although it seems an odd combination, it is delicious.

INGREDIENTS

Serves 4
2½ cups coconut milk
2 tbsp red curry paste
2 tbsp fish sauce
1 tbsp sugar
8oz jumbo shrimp, shelled and deveined
1 lb mussels, cleaned and beards removed
6oz fresh pineapple, finely crushed or chopped
5 kafir lime leaves, torn
2 red chilies, chopped, and cilantro leaves, to garnish

1 In a large saucepan, bring half the coconut milk to a boil and heat, stirring, until it separates.

2 Add the red curry paste and cook until fragrant. Add the fish sauce and sugar and continue to cook for a few moments.

3 Stir in the rest of the coconut milk and bring back to a boil. Add the jumbo shrimp, mussels, pineapple and kafir lime leaves.

4 Reheat until boiling and then simmer for 3–5 minutes, until the shrimp are cooked and the mussels have opened. Remove any mussels that have not opened and discard. Serve garnished with chilies and cilantro.

NUTRITION NOTES	
Per portion:	
Energy	187Kcals/793kJ
Fat	3.5g
Saturated Fat	0.53g
Cholesterol	175.5mg
Fiber	0.59g

CURRIED SHRIMP IN COCONUT MILK

A curry-like dish where the shrimp are cooked in a spicy coconut gravy with sweet and sour flavors from the tomatoes.

INGREDIENTS

Serves 4
2½ cups coconut milk
2 tbsp Thai curry paste
1 tbsp fish sauce
½ tsp salt
1 tsp sugar
1 lb shelled jumbo shrimp, tails left intact and deveined
8oz cherry tomatoes
1 chili, seeded and chopped
juice of ½ lime, to serve
chili and cilantro, to garnish

1 Put half the coconut milk into a pan or wok and bring to a boil.

2 Add the curry paste to the coconut milk, stir until it disperses, then simmer for about 10 minutes.

3 Add the fish sauce, salt, sugar and remaining coconut milk. Simmer for another 5 minutes.

4 Add the shrimp, cherry tomatoes and chili. Simmer gently for about 5 minutes, or until the shrimp are pink and tender.

5 Serve sprinkled with lime juice and garnish with sliced chili and chopped cilantro leaves.

NUTRITION NOTES	
Per portion:	
Energy	184Kcals/778kJ
Fat	3.26g
Saturated fat	0.58g
Cholesterol	315mg
Fiber	0.6g

TUNA AND MIXED VEGETABLE PASTA

INGREDIENTS

Serves 4

2 tsp olive oil
1½ cups button
   mushrooms, sliced
1 garlic clove, crushed
½ red bell pepper, seeded and chopped
1 tbsp tomato paste
1¼ cups tomato juice
1 cup frozen peas
1–2 tbsp drained pickled
   green peppercorns, crushed
12oz whole-wheat pasta shapes
1 7oz can tuna packed in water,
   drained
6 scallions, sliced diagonally

1 Heat the oil in a pan and gently sauté the mushrooms, garlic and pepper until softened. Stir in the tomato paste, then add the tomato juice, peas and some or all of the crushed peppercorns, depending on how spicy you like the sauce. Bring to a boil, lower the heat and simmer.

2 Bring a large saucepan of lightly salted water to a boil and cook the pasta for about 12 minutes (or according to the instructions on the package), until just tender. When the pasta is almost ready, add the tuna to the sauce and heat through gently. Stir in the scallions. Drain the pasta, turn it into a heated bowl and pour on the sauce. Toss to mix. Serve at once.

NUTRITION NOTES

Per portion:

Energy	354Kcals/1514kJ
Fat	4.5g
Saturated fat	0.67g
Cholesterol	22.95mg
Fiber	10.35g

SWEET AND SOUR FISH

White fish is high in protein, vitamins and minerals, but low in fat. Serve this tasty, nutritious dish with brown rice and stir-fried cabbage or spinach for a delicious lunch.

INGREDIENTS

Serves 4

4 tbsp cider vinegar
3 tbsp light soy sauce
¼ cup granulated sugar
1 tbsp tomato paste
1½ tbsp cornstarch
1 cup water
1 green bell pepper, seeded and sliced
1 8oz can pineapple chunks
   in juice
8oz tomatoes, peeled and chopped
2 cups sliced button mushrooms
1½ lb thick haddock fillets,
   skinned
salt and black pepper

1 Preheat the oven to 350°F. Combine the vinegar, soy sauce, sugar and tomato paste in a saucepan. Put the cornstarch in a cup, stir in the water, then add the mixture to the saucepan, stirring well. Bring to a boil, stirring constantly until thickened. Lower the heat and simmer the sauce for 5 minutes.

2 Add the green pepper, canned pineapple chunks (with juice) and tomatoes to the pan and stir well. Mix in the mushrooms and heat through. Season to taste with salt and pepper.

3 Place the fish in a single layer in a shallow ovenproof dish, spoon on the sauce and cover with foil. Bake for 15–20 minutes, until the fish is tender. Serve immediately.

NUTRITION NOTES

Per portion:

Energy	255Kcals/1070kJ
Fat	2g
Saturated fat	0.5g
Cholesterol	61mg

VEGETABLES AND VEGETARIAN DISHES

Vegetarian food provides a tasty and nutritious choice at mealtimes for everyone and is especially tempting when it is low in fat too. Choose from delicious vegetable dishes such as Mixed Mushroom Ragoût, Deviled Onions en Croûte and Zucchini in Citrus Sauce or tempting low fat vegetarian meals such as Autumn Glory, Ratatouille Pancakes, and Tofu and Green Bean Curry.

HERB BAKED TOMATOES

Serves 4–6

1½ lb large red and yellow
    tomatoes
2 tsp red wine vinegar
½ tsp whole-grain mustard
1 garlic clove, crushed
2 tsp chopped fresh parsley
2 tsp chopped fresh chives
½ cup fresh fine white
    bread crumbs, for topping
salt and black pepper

—— **NUTRITION NOTES** ——

Per portion:

Energy	37Kcals/156kJ
Fat	0.49g
Saturated fat	0.16g
Cholesterol	0
Fiber	1.36g

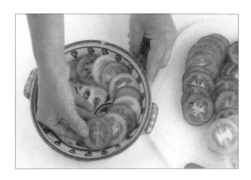

1 Preheat the oven to 400°F. Thickly slice the tomatoes and arrange half of them in a 4 cup ovenproof casserole.

> **COOK'S TIP**
> Use whole-wheat bread crumbs in place of white, for added color, flavor and fiber. Use 1–2 tsp mixed dried herbs, if fresh herbs are not available.

2 Mix the vinegar, mustard, garlic and seasoning together. Stir in 2 teaspoons cold water. Sprinkle the tomatoes with half the parsley and chives, then drizzle with half the dressing.

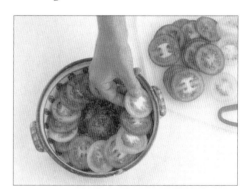

3 Lay the remaining tomato slices on top, overlapping them slightly. Drizzle with the remaining dressing.

4 Sprinkle with the bread crumbs. Bake for 25 minutes or until the topping is golden. Sprinkle with the remaining parsley and chives. Serve immediately, garnished with sprigs of parsley.

POTATO GRATIN

The flavor of Parmesan is wonderfully strong, so a little goes a long way. Leave the cheese out altogether for an almost fat-free dish.

INGREDIENTS

Serves 4
1 garlic clove
5 large baking potatoes, peeled
3 tbsp freshly grated Parmesan cheese
2½ cups vegetable or chicken stock
pinch of grated nutmeg
salt and black pepper

1 Preheat the oven to 400°F. Halve the garlic clove and rub the cut surface over the base and sides of a large shallow gratin dish.

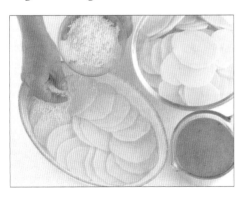

2 Slice the potatoes very thinly and arrange a third of them in the dish. Sprinkle with a little grated Parmesan cheese, and season with salt and pepper. Pour on some of the stock to prevent the potatoes from discoloring.

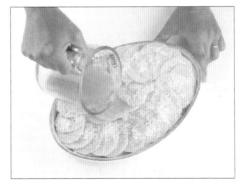

3 Continue layering the potatoes and cheese as before, then add the rest of the stock. Sprinkle with the grated nutmeg.

COOK'S TIP
For a potato and onion gratin, thinly slice one medium onion and layer with the potato.

4 Bake in the preheated oven for 1¼–1½ hours, or until the potatoes are tender and the tops well browned.

NUTRITION NOTES

Per portion:
Energy	178Kcals/749kJ
Protein	9.42g
Fat	1.57g
Saturated fat	0.30g
Fiber	1.82g

MIXED MUSHROOM RAGOÛT

These mushrooms are delicious served hot or cold and can be prepared up to two days in advance.

INGREDIENTS

Serves 4

1 small onion, finely chopped
1 garlic clove, crushed
1 tbsp coriander seeds, crushed
2 tbsp red wine vinegar
1 tbsp soy sauce
1 tbsp dry sherry
2 tsp tomato paste
2 tsp light brown sugar
⅔ cup vegetable stock
4oz baby button mushrooms
4oz chestnut mushrooms,
   quartered
4oz oyster mushrooms, sliced
salt and black pepper
cilantro sprig, to garnish

NUTRITION NOTES

Per portion:

Energy	41Kcals/172kJ
Protein	2.51g
Fat	0.66g
Saturated fat	0.08g
Fiber	1.02g

COOK'S TIP
There are many types of fresh mushrooms available and all are low in calories and fat. They add flavor and color to many low fat dishes such as this tasty ragoût.

1 Put the first nine ingredients in a large saucepan. Bring to a boil and reduce the heat. Cover and simmer for 5 minutes.

2 Uncover the saucepan and simmer for 5 more minutes, or until the liquid has reduced by half.

3 Add the baby button and chestnut mushrooms and simmer for 3 minutes. Stir in the oyster mushrooms and cook for another 2 minutes.

4 Remove the mushrooms from the pan with a slotted spoon and transfer them to a serving dish. Keep warm, if serving hot.

5 Boil the juices for about 5 minutes, or until reduced to about 5 tablespoons. Season to taste.

6 Allow to cool for 2–3 minutes, then pour on the mushrooms. Serve hot or well chilled, garnished with a sprig of cilantro.

DEVILED ONIONS EN CROÛTE

Fill crisp bread cups with tender button onions tossed in a mustard glaze. Try other low fat mixtures of vegetables, such as ratatouille, for a delicious change.

INGREDIENTS

Serves 4

12 thin slices of white or
  whole-wheat bread
8oz button onions or shallots
1²⁄₃ cup vegetable stock
1 tbsp dry white wine or
  dry sherry
2 turkey bacon strips, cut into thin strips
2 tsp Worcestershire sauce
1 tsp tomato paste
¹⁄₄ tsp prepared mustard
salt and black pepper
sprigs of flat leaf parsley, to garnish

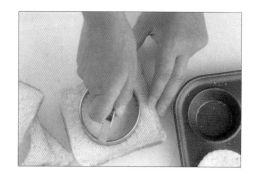

1 Preheat the oven to 400°F. Cut the bread into rounds with a 3in fluted biscuit cutter and use to line a 12 cup muffin tin.

2 Cover each bread case with non-stick baking paper and fill with baking beans or weights. Bake for 5 minutes. Remove the paper and beans and bake for another 5 minutes, until lightly browned and crisp.

3 Meanwhile, put the button onions or shallots in a bowl and cover with boiling water. Let stand for 3 minutes, then drain and rinse under cold water. Trim off their top and root ends and slip them out of their skins.

4 Simmer the onions and stock in a covered saucepan for 5 minutes. Uncover and cook, stirring occasionally, until the stock has reduced entirely. Add all the remaining ingredients, except the flat leaf parsley, and cook for 2–3 minutes.

5 Fill the toast cups with the deviled onions. Serve hot, garnished with sprigs of flat leaf parsley.

NUTRITION NOTES	
Per portion:	
Energy	178Kcals/749kJ
Protein	9.42g
Fat	1.57g
Saturated fat	0.30g
Fiber	1.82g

KOHLRABI STUFFED WITH PEPPERS

If you haven't sampled kohlrabi, or have only eaten it in stews where its flavor is lost, this dish is recommended. The slightly sharp flavor of the peppers are an excellent foil to the more earthy flavor of the kohlrabi.

INGREDIENTS

Serves 4

4 small kohlrabies, about
  6–8 ounces each
about ⅔ cup hot vegetable stock
1 tbsp sunflower oil
1 onion, chopped
1 small red and 1 small green bell
  pepper, seeded and sliced
salt and black pepper
sprigs of flat leaf parsley, to garnish
  (optional)

NUTRITION NOTES

Per portion:	
Energy	112Kcals/470kJ
Fat	4.63g
Saturated fat	0.55g
Cholesterol	0
Fiber	5.8g

1 Preheat the oven to 350°F. Trim and remove the ends of the kohlrabies and arrange in the base of a medium-sized ovenproof dish.

2 Add the stock to come about halfway up the vegetables. Cover and braise in the oven for about 30 minutes, until tender. Transfer to a plate and allow to cool, reserving the stock.

3 Heat the oil in a frying pan and fry the onion for 3–4 minutes over gentle heat, stirring occasionally. Add the peppers and cook for another 2–3 minutes, until the onion is lightly browned.

4 Add the reserved vegetable stock and a little seasoning and simmer, uncovered, over medium heat until the stock has almost evaporated.

5 Scoop out the insides of the kohlrabies and chop coarsely. Stir into the onion and pepper mixture, taste and adjust the seasoning. Arrange the shells in a shallow ovenproof dish.

6 Spoon the filling into the kohlrabi shells. Put in the oven for 5–10 minutes to heat through and then serve, garnished with a sprig of flat leaf parsley, if desired.

ZUCCHINI IN CITRUS SAUCE

If baby zucchini are unavailable, you can use larger ones, but they should be cooked whole, so that they don't absorb too much water. After cooking, halve them lengthwise and cut into 4-inch lengths. These tender, baby zucchini served in a very low fat sauce make this a tasty and low fat accompaniment to grilled fish fillets.

NUTRITION NOTES

Per portion:

Energy	33Kcals/138kJ
Protein	2.18g
Fat	0.42g
Saturated fat	0.09g
Fiber	0.92g

INGREDIENTS

Serves 4

12oz baby zucchini
4 scallions, finely sliced
1in piece fresh ginger, grated
2 tbsp cider vinegar
1 tbsp light soy sauce
1 tsp light brown sugar
3 tbsp vegetable stock
finely grated rind and juice of ½ lemon
    and ½ orange
1 tsp cornstarch

2 Meanwhile, put all the remaining ingredients, except the cornstarch, into a small saucepan and bring to a boil. Simmer for 3 minutes.

3 Blend the cornstarch with 2 tsp cold water and add to the sauce. Bring to a boil, stirring constantly, until the sauce has thickened.

1 Cook the zucchini in lightly salted boiling water for 3–4 minutes or until just tender. Drain well.

4 Pour the sauce over the zucchini and heat gently, shaking the pan to coat them evenly. Transfer to a warmed serving dish and serve.

COOK'S TIP
Use baby corn or eggplant in place of the zucchini for an appetizing change.

ZUCCHINI AND ASPARAGUS PACKAGES

To appreciate the aroma, these paper packages should be broken open at the table.

INGREDIENTS

Serves 4
2 medium zucchini
1 medium leek
8oz young asparagus, trimmed
4 tarragon sprigs
4 whole garlic cloves, unpeeled
1 egg, beaten, to glaze
salt and black pepper

NUTRITION NOTES

Per portion:
Energy	110Kcals/460kJ
Protein	6.22g
Fat	2.29g
Saturated fat	0.49g
Fiber	6.73g

1 Preheat the oven to 400°F. Using a potato peeler, carefully slice the zucchini lengthwise into thin strips.

2 Cut the leek into very fine julienne strips and cut the asparagus evenly into 2in lengths.

3 Cut out four sheets of parchment paper measuring 12 x 15 in and fold in half. Draw a large curve to make a heart shape when unfolded. Cut along the inside of the line and open out.

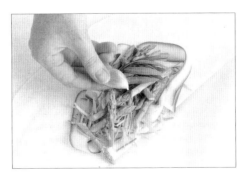

4 Divide the zucchini, asparagus and leek evenly between each paper heart, positioning the filling on one side of the fold line, and topping each with a sprig of tarragon and an unpeeled garlic clove. Season to taste.

5 Brush the edges lightly with the beaten egg and fold over.

6 Twist the edges together so that each package is completely sealed. Lay the packages on a baking sheet and cook for 10 minutes. Serve immediately.

COOK'S TIP
Experiment with other vegetable combinations, if desired.

AUTUMN GLORY

Glorious pumpkin shells summon up the delights of autumn and look too good to throw away, so use one as a serving pot. Pumpkin and pasta make great partners, especially as a main course served from the baked shell.

INGREDIENTS

Serves 4–6
1 pumpkin, about 4–4½ lb
1 onion, sliced
1in piece fresh ginger
1 tbsp extra virgin olive oil
1 zucchini, sliced
1¾ cups sliced mushrooms
1 14oz chopped tomatoes
1 cup pasta shells
2 cups stock
4 tbsp ricotta cheese
2 tbsp chopped fresh basil
salt and black pepper

NUTRITION NOTES

Per portion (for 6):
Energy	140Kcals/588kJ
Fat	4.29g
Saturated fat	1.17g
Cholesterol	2.5mg
Fiber	4.45g

COOK'S TIP

Use reduced-fat or very low fat ricotta cheese to cut the calories and fat. Cook the onion, ginger and pumpkin flesh in 2–3 tbsp vegetable stock in place of the oil, to cut the calories and fat even more.

1 Preheat the oven to 350°F. Cut the top off the pumpkin with a large sharp knife, then scoop out and discard the seeds.

2 Using a small sharp knife and a sturdy tablespoon, extract as much of the pumpkin flesh as possible, then chop it into chunks.

3 Bake the pumpkin shell with its lid on for 45 minutes to 1 hour, until the inside begins to soften.

4 Meanwhile make the filling. Gently fry the onion, ginger and pumpkin chunks in the olive oil for about 10 minutes, stirring occasionally.

5 Add the zucchini and mushrooms and cook for another 3 minutes, then stir in the tomatoes, pasta shells and stock. Season well, bring to a boil, then cover and simmer gently for another 10 minutes.

6 Stir the ricotta cheese and basil into the pasta and spoon the mixture into the pumpkin. (It may not be possible to fit all the filling into the pumpkin shell; serve the rest separately if this is the case.)

VEGETABLES À LA GRECQUE

This simple side salad is made with winter vegetables, but you can vary it according to the season. This combination of vegetables makes an ideal, low fat side salad to serve with grilled lean meat or poultry, or with thick slices of fresh, crusty bread.

INGREDIENTS

Serves 4

¾ cup white wine
1 tsp olive oil
2 tbsp lemon juice
2 bay leaves
sprig of fresh thyme
4 juniper berries
1 lb leeks, cut into 1in lengths
1 small cauliflower, broken into florets
4 celery stalks, sliced on the diagonal
2 tbsp chopped fresh parsley
salt and black pepper

1 Put the wine, oil, lemon juice, bay leaves, thyme and juniper berries into a large, heavy saucepan and bring to a boil. Cover and let simmer for 20 minutes.

NUTRITION NOTES

Per portion:

Energy	88Kcals/368kJ
Protein	4.53g
Fat	2.05g
Saturated fat	0.11g
Fiber	4.42g

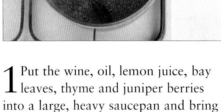

2 Add the leeks, cauliflower and celery. Simmer very gently for 5–6 minutes, or until just tender.

3 Remove the vegetables with a slotted spoon and transfer them to a serving dish. Briskly boil the cooking liquid for 15–20 minutes, or until reduced by half. Strain.

4 Stir the parsley into the liquid and season with salt and pepper to taste. Pour over the vegetables and allow to cool. Chill in the fridge for at least 1 hour before serving.

COOK'S TIP
Choose a dry or medium-dry white wine for best results.

ROASTED MEDITERRANEAN VEGETABLES

For a really colorful dish, try these vegetables roasted in olive oil with garlic and rosemary. The flavor is wonderfully intense.

INGREDIENTS

Serves 6

1 each red and yellow bell pepper
2 Spanish onions
2 large zucchini
1 large eggplant or 4 baby eggplant,
  trimmed
1 fennel bulb, thickly sliced
2 beefsteak tomatoes
8 fat garlic cloves
2 tbsp olive oil
fresh rosemary sprigs
black pepper
lemon wedges and black olives
  (optional), to garnish

1 Halve and seed the peppers, then cut them into large chunks. Peel the onions and cut into thick wedges.

NUTRITION NOTES

Per portion:	
Energy	120Kcals/504kJ
Fat	5.2g
Saturated fat	0.68g
Cholesterol	0

2 Cut the zucchini and eggplant into large chunks.

3 Preheat the oven to 425°F. Spread the peppers, onions, zucchini, eggplant and fennel in a lightly oiled shallow ovenproof dish or roasting pan, or, if desired, arrange in rows to make a colorful design.

4 Cut each tomato in half and place, cut-side up, with the vegetables.

5 Tuck the garlic cloves among the vegetables, then brush them with the olive oil. Place some sprigs of rosemary among the vegetables and grind some black pepper over the top, particularly on the tomatoes.

6 Roast for 20–25 minutes, turning the vegetables halfway through the cooking time. Serve from the dish or on a flat platter, garnished with lemon wedges. Scatter some black olives over the top, if desired.

RATATOUILLE PANCAKES

These pancakes are made slightly thicker than usual to hold the juicy vegetable filling. By using cooking spray, you can control the amount of fat you are using and keep it to a minimum.

INGREDIENTS

Serves 4

⅔ cup all-purpose flour
pinch of salt
¼ cup quick-cooking oatmeal
1 egg
1¼ cups skim milk
nonstick cooking spray
mixed salad, to serve

For the filling

1 large eggplant, cut into
 1in cubes
1 garlic clove, crushed
2 medium zucchini, sliced
1 green bell pepper, seeded and sliced
1 red bell pepper, seeded and sliced
5 tbsp vegetable stock
1 7oz can chopped tomatoes
1 teaspoon cornstarch
salt and black pepper

NUTRITION NOTES

Per portion:

Energy	182Kcals/767kJ
Protein	9.36g
Fat	3.07g
Saturated fat	0.62g
Fiber	4.73g

COOK'S TIP
Adding oatmeal to the batter mixture adds flavor, color and texture to the cooked pancakes. If desired, use whole-wheat flour in place of white flour to add extra fiber and flavor.

1 Sift the flour and a pinch of salt into a bowl. Stir in the oats. Make a well in the center, add the egg and half the milk and mix to a smooth batter. Gradually beat in the remaining milk. Cover the bowl and allow to stand for 30 minutes.

2 Spray a 7in heavy pan with cooking spray. Heat the pan, then pour in just enough batter to cover the bottom of the pan thinly. Cook for 2–3 minutes, until the underside is golden brown. Flip over and cook for another 1–2 minutes.

3 Slide the pancake out onto a plate lined with nonstick baking paper. Stack the other pancakes on top as they are made, interleaving each with parchment paper. Keep warm.

4 For the filling, put the eggplant in a colander and sprinkle well with salt. Let stand on a plate for 30 minutes. Rinse thoroughly and drain well.

5 Put the garlic clove, zucchini, peppers, stock and tomatoes into a large saucepan. Simmer uncovered, stirring occasionally, for 10 minutes. Add the eggplant and cook for another 15 minutes. Blend the cornstarch with 2 teaspoons water and stir into the saucepan. Simmer for 2 minutes. Season to taste.

6 Spoon some of the ratatouille mixture into the middle of each pancake. Fold each one in half, then in half again to make a cone shape. Serve hot with a mixed salad.

Baked Garlic Potatoes

With a low fat topping these would make a superb meal in themselves or could be enjoyed as a nutritious accompaniment to grilled fish or meat.

Serves 4
4 *baking potatoes*
2 *garlic cloves, cut into slivers*
4 *tbsp low fat ricotta cheese*
4 *tbsp low fat plain yogurt*
2 *tbsp snipped chives*
6–8 *watercress sprigs, finely chopped*
(optional)

─────── **Nutrition Notes** ───────

Per portion:
Energy	195Kcals/815kJ
Fat	3.5g
Saturated fat	2g
Cholesterol	10mg

1 Preheat the oven to 400°F. Slice each potato at about ¼in intervals, cutting not quite to the base, so that they retain their shape. Slip the slivers of the garlic between the cuts in the potatoes.

> **Cook's Tip**
> If available, farmer's cheese or low fat cream cheese are very good substitutes for the ricotta cheese.

2 Place the garlic-filled potatoes in a roasting tin and bake for 1–1¼ hours, or until soft when tested with a knife. Meanwhile, mix the low fat ricotta cheese and yogurt in a bowl, then stir in the snipped chives, along with the watercress, if using.

3 Serve the baked potatoes on individual plates, with a dollop of the yogurt and ricotta cheese mixture on top of each.

Potato, Leek and Tomato Tian

Serves 4
1½ *lb potatoes*
2 *leeks, sliced*
3 *large tomatoes, sliced*
a few fresh rosemary sprigs, crushed
1 *garlic clove, crushed*
1¼ *cups vegetable stock*
1 *tbsp olive oil*
salt and black pepper

─────── **Nutrition Notes** ───────

Per portion:
Energy	180Kcals/740kJ
Fat	3.5g
Saturated fat	0.5g
Cholesterol	0

1 Preheat the oven to 350°F and grease a 5-cup shallow ovenproof dish. Scrub and thinly slice the potatoes. Alternately layer them with the leeks and tomatoes in the dish, sprinkling some rosemary between the layers and ending with a layer of potatoes.

2 Add the garlic to the stock, stir in salt if needed and pepper to taste, then add to the vegetables. Brush the top layer of potatoes with olive oil.

3 Bake for 1¼–1½ hours, until the potatoes are tender and the topping is golden and slightly crisp.

MUSHROOM AND OKRA CURRY

This simple but delicious curry with its fresh gingery mango relish is best served with plain basmati rice.

INGREDIENTS

Serves 4

4 garlic cloves, coarsely chopped
1in piece fresh ginger, peeled and coarsely chopped
1–2 red chilies, seeded and chopped
¾ cup cold water
1 tbsp sunflower oil
1 tsp coriander seeds
1 tsp cumin seeds
1 tsp ground cumin
2 cardamom pods, seeds removed and crushed
pinch of ground turmeric
1 14oz can chopped tomatoes
1 lb mushrooms, quartered if large
8oz okra, trimmed and cut into ½ in slices
2 tbsp chopped cilantro
basmati rice, to serve

For the mango relish
1 large ripe mango, about 1¼ lb
1 small garlic clove, crushed
1 onion, finely chopped
2 tsp grated fresh ginger
1 fresh red chili, seeded and finely chopped
pinch of salt and sugar

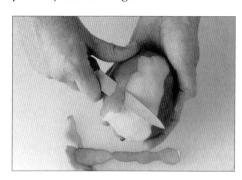

1 For the mango relish, peel the mango and then cut off the fruit from the pit. Put the mango into a bowl and mash with a fork, or use a food processor.

2 Add the rest of the relish ingredients to the mashed mango, mix well and set aside.

3 Place the garlic, ginger, chilies and 3 tbsp of the water into a blender and blend until smooth. Heat the sunflower oil in a large pan. Add the coriander and cumin seeds and allow them to sizzle for a few seconds. Add the ground cumin, cardamom and turmeric and cook for 1 more minute.

4 Add the paste from the blender, the tomatoes, remaining water, mushrooms and okra. Stir to mix well and bring to a boil. Reduce the heat, cover and simmer for 5 minutes. Uncover, turn up the heat slightly and cook for another 5–10 minutes, until the okra is tender. Stir in the cilantro and serve with rice and the mango relish.

NUTRITION NOTES	
Per portion:	
Energy	139Kcals/586kJ
Fat	4.6g
Saturated fat	0.63g
Cholesterol	0
Fiber	6.96g

TOFU AND GREEN BEAN CURRY

This exotic curry is simple and quick to make. This recipe uses beans and mushrooms, but you can use almost any kind of vegetable, such as eggplant, bamboo shoots or broccoli.

INGREDIENTS

Serves 4

1½ cups coconut milk
1 tbsp red curry paste
3 tbsp fish sauce
2 tsp sugar
8oz button mushrooms
4oz green beans, trimmed
6oz tofu, rinsed and cut into
  ¾in cubes
4 kafir lime leaves, torn
2 red chilies, seeded and sliced
cilantro leaves, to garnish

NUTRITION NOTES

Per portion:	
Energy	100Kcals/420kJ
Fat	3.36g
Saturated fat	0.48g
Cholesterol	0
Fiber	1.35g

1 Put about one third of the coconut milk in a wok or saucepan. Cook until it starts to separate and an oily sheen appears.

2 Add the red curry paste, fish sauce and sugar to the coconut milk. Mix together thoroughly.

3 Add the mushrooms. Stir and cook for 1 minute.

4 Stir in the rest of the coconut milk and bring back to a boil.

COOK'S TIP
Use 1–2 tsp hot chili powder, if fresh red chilies aren't available. When preparing fresh chilies, wear rubber gloves and wash hands, work surfaces and utensils thoroughly afterwards. Chilies contain volatile oils which can irritate and burn sensitive areas, especially eyes.

5 Add the green beans and cubes of tofu and simmer gently for another 4–5 minutes.

6 Stir in the kafir lime leaves and chilies. Serve garnished with the cilantro leaves.

VEGETARIAN CASSOULET

Every town in southwest France has its own version of this popular classic. Warm French bread is all that you need to accompany this hearty low fat vegetable version.

INGREDIENTS

Serves 4–6

2 cups dried navy beans
1 bay leaf
2 onions
3 whole cloves
2 garlic cloves, crushed
1 tsp olive oil
2 leeks, thickly sliced
12 baby carrots
4oz button mushrooms
1 14oz can chopped tomatoes
1 tbsp tomato paste
1 tsp paprika
1 tbsp chopped fresh thyme
2 tbsp chopped fresh parsley
2 cups fresh white
  bread crumbs
salt and black pepper

NUTRITION NOTES

Per portion:

Energy	325Kcals/1378kJ
Fat	3.08g
Saturated Fat	0.46g
Cholesterol	0
Fiber	15.68g

COOK'S TIP

If you're short of time, use canned navy beans – you'll need two 14oz cans. Drain, reserving the bean juices and bring up to 1²/₃ cups with vegetable stock.

1 Soak the beans overnight in plenty of cold water. Drain and rinse under cold running water. Put them in a saucepan with 7½ cups of cold water and the bay leaf. Bring to a boil and cook rapidly for 10 minutes.

2 Peel one of the onions and spike with the cloves. Add to the beans, then reduce the heat. Cover and simmer gently for 1 hour, until the beans are almost tender. Drain, reserving the stock but discarding the bay leaf and onion.

3 Chop the remaining onion and put it into a large flameproof casserole together with the crushed garlic and olive oil. Cook gently for 5 minutes, or until softened.

4 Preheat the oven to 325°F. Add the leeks, carrots, mushrooms, chopped tomatoes, tomato paste, paprika and thyme to the casserole, then pour in about 1²/₃ cups of the reserved stock.

5 Bring to a boil, cover and simmer gently for 10 minutes. Stir in the cooked beans and parsley. Season to taste with salt and pepper.

6 Sprinkle the bread crumbs over the top and bake uncovered for 35 minutes, or until the topping is golden brown and crisp.

SALADS

Salads are healthy and refreshing and can be served either as accompaniments to other dishes or as perfect low fat meals in themselves. Presented here is a wonderful selection of recipes: vegetarian delights include Marinated Cucumber Salad and a fresh, fast and filling Fruit and Fiber Salad; there are fish and seafood dishes, such as Shrimp Noodle Salad and a tasty Thai-style Seafood Salad with Fragrant Herbs; and healthy salads made with grains and rice, such as Bulgur Salad with Oranges and Brown Rice Salad with Fruit, which are hearty enough to serve as a meal on their own.

MARINATED CUCUMBER SALAD

Sprinkling cucumbers with salt draws out some of the water and makes them softer and sweeter.

INGREDIENTS

Serves 6

2 medium cucumbers
1 tbsp salt
½ cup sugar
¾ cup dry cider
1 tbsp cider vinegar
3 tbsp chopped fresh dill
pinch of pepper

NUTRITION NOTES

Per portion:
Energy	111Kcals/465kJ
Fat	0.14g
Saturated fat	0.01g
Fiber	0.62g

1 Slice the cucumbers thinly and place them in a colander, sprinkling salt between each layer. Put the colander over a bowl and set aside to drain for 1 hour.

> **COOK'S TIP**
> As a shortcut, leave out the method for salting cucumber described in step 1.

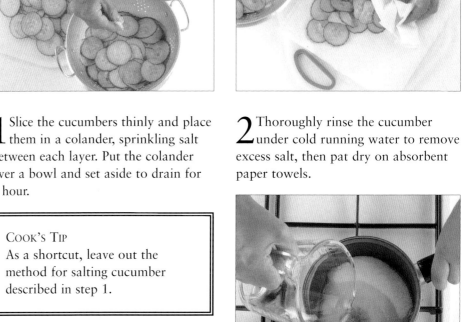

2 Thoroughly rinse the cucumber under cold running water to remove excess salt, then pat dry on absorbent paper towels.

3 Gently heat the sugar, cider and vinegar in a saucepan, until the sugar has dissolved. Remove from the heat and allow to cool. Put the cucumber slices in a bowl, pour the cider mixture over them and allow to marinate for about 2 hours.

4 Drain the cucumber and sprinkle with the dill and pepper to taste. Mix well and transfer to a serving dish. Chill in the fridge until ready to serve.

TURNIP SALAD WITH HORSERADISH

The robust-flavored turnip partners well with the taste of horseradish and caraway seeds. This salad is delicious with cold roast beef or smoked trout.

INGREDIENTS

Serves 4

12oz medium turnips
2 scallions, white part only, chopped
1 tbsp sugar
salt
2 tbsp creamed horseradish
2 tsp caraway seeds

NUTRITION NOTES

Per portion:

Energy	48.25Kcals/204kJ
Fat	1.26g
Saturated fat	0.09g
Cholesterol	1mg
Fiber	2.37g

1 Peel, slice and shred the turnips – or grate them if desired.

> **COOK'S TIP**
> If turnips are not available, giant white radish (daikon) can be used as a substitute. For extra sweetness, try red onion instead of scallions.

2 Add the scallions, sugar and salt, then rub together with your hands to soften the turnip.

3 Fold in the creamed horseradish and caraway seeds and serve.

FRUIT AND FIBER SALAD

Fresh, fast and filling, this salad makes a great supper or snack.

INGREDIENTS

Serves 6
8oz red or white cabbage, or a mixture of both
3 medium carrots
1 pear
1 red-skinned eating apple
1 7oz can cannellini beans, drained
¼ cup chopped dates

For the dressing
½ tsp dry English mustard
2 tsp honey
2 tbsp orange juice
1 tsp white wine vinegar
½ tsp paprika
salt and black pepper

1 Shred the cabbage very finely, discarding the core and tough ribs.

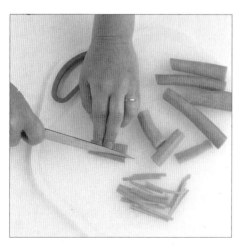

2 Cut the carrots into very thin strips, about 2in long.

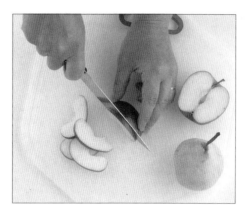

3 Quarter, core and slice the pear and the apple, leaving the peel on.

4 Put the fruit and vegetables in a bowl with the beans and dates. Mix well.

5 To make the dressing, blend the mustard with the honey until smooth. Add the orange juice, vinegar, paprika and seasoning and mix well.

6 Pour the dressing over the salad and toss to coat. Chill in the fridge for 30 minutes before serving.

NUTRITION NOTES

Per portion:

Energy	137Kcals/574kJ
Fat	0.87g
Saturated fat	0.03g
Fiber	6.28g

COOK'S TIP
Use other canned beans, such as red kidney beans or chickpeas, in place of the cannellini beans. Add ½ tsp ground spice, such as chili powder, cumin or coriander, for extra flavor. Add 1 tsp finely grated orange or lemon rind to the dressing, for extra flavor.

EGGPLANT SALAD

An appetizing and unusual salad that you will find yourself making over and over again.

INGREDIENTS

Serves 6
2 eggplant
1 tbsp oil
2 tbsp dried shrimp, soaked
  and drained
1 tbsp coarsely chopped garlic
2 tbsp fresh lime juice
1 tsp sugar
2 tbsp fish sauce
1 hard-cooked egg, chopped
4 shallots, thinly sliced into rings
cilantro leaves, to garnish
2 red chilies, seeded and sliced,
  to garnish

COOK'S TIP
For an interesting variation, if available, try using salted duck's or quail's eggs, cut in half, instead of chopped hen's eggs.

1 Grill or roast the eggplant until charred and tender.

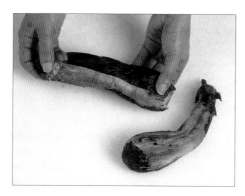

2 When cool enough to handle, peel away the skin and slice the eggplant into thick pieces.

3 Heat the oil in a small frying pan, add the drained shrimp and the garlic and fry until golden. Remove from the pan and set aside.

4 To make the dressing, put the lime juice, sugar and fish sauce in a small bowl and whisk together.

5 To serve, arrange the eggplant on a serving dish. Top with the chopped egg, shallot rings and dried shrimp mixture. Drizzle on the dressing and garnish with cilantro and red chilies.

NUTRITION NOTES

Per portion:

Energy	70.5Kcals/295kJ
Fat	3.76g
Saturated fat	0.68g
Cholesterol	57mg
Fiber	1.20g

BAMBOO SHOOT SALAD

This salad, which has a hot and sharp flavor, originated in north-east Thailand. Use fresh young bamboo shoots if you can find them, otherwise substitute canned bamboo shoots.

INGREDIENTS

Serves 4
1 14oz can whole bamboo shoots
1oz glutinous rice
2 tbsp chopped shallots
1 tbsp chopped garlic
3 tbsp chopped scallions
2 tbsp fish sauce
2 tbsp lime juice
1 tsp sugar
½ tsp dried flaked chilies
20–25 small mint leaves
1 tbsp toasted sesame seeds

1 Rinse and drain the bamboo shoots, then slice and set aside.

2 Dry roast the rice in a frying pan until it is golden brown. Remove and grind to fine crumbs with a mortar and pestle.

3 Transfer the rice to a bowl, add the shallots, garlic, scallions, fish sauce, lime juice, sugar, chilies and half the mint leaves.

4 Mix thoroughly, then add the bamboo shoots and toss together. Serve sprinkled with sesame seeds and the remaining mint leaves.

COOK'S TIP
Omit the sesame seeds to reduce calories and fat. Use prepared minced garlic instead of crushing your own.

NUTRITION NOTES

Per portion:	
Energy	73.5Kcals/308kJ
Fat	2.8g
Saturated fat	0.41g
Cholesterol	0
Fiber	2.45g

BULGUR SALAD WITH ORANGES

Bulgur makes an excellent alternative to rice or pasta.

INGREDIENTS

Serves 6
1 small green bell pepper
1 cup bulgur
½ cucumber, diced
½ cup chopped fresh mint
⅓ cup flaked almonds, toasted
grated rind and juice of 1 lemon
2 seedless oranges
salt and black pepper
mint sprigs, to garnish

1 Using a sharp vegetable knife, carefully halve and seed the green pepper. Cut it on a board into small cubes and put to one side.

2 Place the bulgur in a saucepan and add 2½ cups water. Bring to a boil, lower the heat, cover and simmer for 10–15 minutes, until tender. Alternatively, place the bulgur in a heatproof bowl, add boiling water and allow to soak for 30 minutes. Most, if not all, of the water should be absorbed; drain off any excess.

3 Toss the bulgur with the cucumber, green pepper, mint and toasted almonds in a serving bowl. Add the grated lemon rind and juice.

4 Cut the rind from the oranges, then working over the bowl to catch the juice, cut the oranges into neat segments. Add to the bulgur mixture, then season and toss lightly. Garnish with the mint sprigs.

NUTRITION NOTES

Per portion:
Energy	160Kcals/672kJ
Fat	4.3g
Saturated fat	0.33g
Cholesterol	0

BROWN RICE SALAD WITH FRUIT

An Asian-style dressing gives this colorful rice salad extra piquancy. Whole grains like brown rice are unrefined, so they retain their natural fiber, vitamins and minerals.

INGREDIENTS

Serves 4–6

⅔ *cup brown rice*
1 small red bell pepper, seeded and diced
1 7oz can corn niblets, drained
3 tbsp golden raisins
1 8oz can pineapple pieces in juice
1 tbsp light soy sauce
1 tsp sunflower oil
2 tsp hazelnut oil
1 garlic clove, crushed
1 tsp minced fresh ginger
ground black pepper
4 scallions, sliced, to garnish

COOK'S TIP
Hazelnut oil, which contains mainly monounsaturated fats, adds a wonderful flavor.

1 Cook the brown rice in a large saucepan of lightly salted boiling water for about 30 minutes, or until it is tender. Drain thoroughly and cool. Meanwhile, prepare the garnish by slicing the scallions at an angle and setting aside.

2 Transfer the rice to a bowl and add the red pepper, corn and raisins. Drain the pineapple pieces, reserving the juice, add them to the rice mixture and toss lightly.

3 Pour the reserved pineapple juice into a clean screw-top jar. Add the soy sauce, sunflower and hazelnut oils, garlic and ginger. Add some salt and pepper, then close the jar tightly and shake well to combine.

4 Pour the dressing over the salad and toss well. Sprinkle the scallions over the top.

NUTRITION NOTES

Per portion:	
Energy	245Kcals/1029kJ
Fat	4.25g
Saturated fat	0.6g
Cholesterol	0

SEAFOOD SALAD WITH FRAGRANT HERBS

Serves 6

1 cup fish stock or water
12oz squid, cleaned and cut
 into rings
12 uncooked jumbo shrimp, shelled
12 scallops
2oz bean thread noodles, soaked in
 warm water for 30 minutes
½ cucumber, cut into thin sticks
1 lemongrass stalk, finely chopped
2 kafir lime leaves, finely shredded
2 shallots, finely sliced
juice of 1–2 limes
2 tbsp fish sauce
2 tbsp chopped scallions
2 tbsp chopped cilantro leaves
12–15 mint leaves, roughly torn
4 red chilies, seeded and sliced
cilantro sprigs, to garnish

1 Pour the stock or water into a medium saucepan, set over high heat and bring to a boil.

2 Cook each type of seafood separately in the stock. Don't overcook – it takes only a few minutes for each. Remove and set aside.

3 Drain the bean thread noodles and cut them into short lengths, about 2in long. Combine the noodles with the cooked seafood.

4 Add all the remaining ingredients, stir well and serve garnished with cilantro sprigs.

Per portion:

Energy	78Kcals/332kJ
Fat	1.12g
Saturated fat	0.26g
Cholesterol	123mg
Fiber	0.37g

COOK'S TIP
Use other prepared seafood, such as mussels and crabmeat, in place of the shrimp or scallops. If fresh chilies are not available, use 2–3 tsp of hot ground chilies or, alternatively, use dried chopped chilies.

GREEN PAPAYA SALAD

There are many variations of this salad in southeast Asia. Because green papaya is not easy to find, shredded carrots, cucumber or green apple may be substituted. Serve this salad with raw white cabbage and rice.

INGREDIENTS

Serves 4

1 medium green papaya
4 garlic cloves
1 tbsp chopped shallots
3–4 red chilies, seeded and sliced
½ tsp salt
2–3 green beans, cut into
  ¾ in lengths
2 tomatoes, cut into wedges
3 tbsp fish sauce
1 tbsp sugar
juice of 1 lime
2 tbsp crushed roasted peanuts
sliced red chilies, to garnish

1 Peel the papaya and cut in half lengthwise, scrape out the seeds with a spoon and finely shred the flesh.

2 Grind the garlic, shallots, chilies and salt together in a large mortar and pestle.

3 Add the shredded papaya a little at a time and pound until it becomes slightly limp and soft.

4 Add the sliced beans and tomatoes and lightly crush. Season with fish sauce, sugar and lime juice.

5 Transfer the salad to a serving dish, sprinkle with crushed peanuts and garnish with chilies.

NUTRITION NOTES

Per portion:

Energy	96Kcals/402kJ
Fat	4.2g
Saturated fat	0.77g
Cholesterol	0

COOK'S TIP
If you do not have a large mortar and pestle, use a bowl and crush the shredded papaya with a wooden meat pounder or the end of a rolling pin.

THAI-STYLE CHICKEN SALAD

This salad comes from Chiang Mai, a city in the northeast of Thailand. It's hot and spicy, and wonderfully aromatic. Choose strong-flavored leaves, such as curly endive or arugula, for the salad.

INGREDIENTS

Serves 6
1 lb ground chicken breast
1 lemongrass stalk, finely chopped
3 kafir lime leaves, finely chopped
4 red chilies, seeded and chopped
4 tbsp lime juice
2 tbsp fish sauce
1 tbsp roasted ground rice
2 scallions, chopped
2 tbsp cilantro leaves
mixed salad leaves, cucumber and
*   tomato slices, to serve*
mint sprigs, to garnish

1 Heat a large nonstick frying pan. Add the ground chicken and cook in a little water.

2 Stir constantly until cooked, which will take about 7–10 minutes.

3 Transfer the cooked chicken to a large bowl and add the rest of the ingredients. Mix thoroughly.

4 Serve on a bed of mixed salad leaves, cucumber and tomato slices, garnished with mint sprigs.

COOK'S TIP
Use sticky (glutinous) rice to make roasted ground rice. Put the rice in a frying pan and dry-roast until golden brown. Remove and grind to a powder with a mortar and pestle or in a food processor. Keep in a glass jar in a cool dry place and use as needed.

NUTRITION NOTES

Per portion:

Energy	106Kcals/446kJ
Fat	1.13g
Saturated fat	0.28g
Cholesterol	52.5mg
Fiber	0.7g

FRUIT, PASTA AND SHRIMP SALAD

Orange cantaloupe and Cassava melons look spectacular in this salad. Or try a mixture of honeydew, cantaloupe and watermelon.

INGREDIENTS

Serves 6
6oz pasta shapes
2 cups cooked shrimp
1 large or 2 small melons
2 tbsp olive oil
1 tbsp tarragon vinegar
*2 tbsp chopped fresh chives or chopped
    parsley*
herb sprigs, to garnish
shredded Chinese cabbage, to serve

NUTRITION NOTES

Per portion:	
Energy	167Kcals/705kJ
Fat	4.72g
Saturated fat	0.68g
Cholesterol	105mg
Fiber	2.08g

1 Cook the pasta in boiling salted water according to the instructions on the package. Drain well and allow to cool.

COOK'S TIP
Use whole-wheat pasta in place of white pasta, and mussels or scallops in place of shrimp.

2 Peel the shrimp and discard the shells.

3 Halve the melon(s) and remove the seeds with a teaspoon. Scoop the flesh into balls with a melon baller and mix with the shrimp and pasta.

4 Whisk the oil, vinegar and chopped herbs together. Pour onto the shrimp mixture and turn to coat. Cover and chill for at least 30 minutes.

5 Meanwhile, shred the Chinese cabbage and use to line a shallow bowl or the empty melon shells. Pile the shrimp mixture onto the Chinese cabbage and garnish with herb sprigs.

SHRIMP NOODLE SALAD

A light, refreshing salad with all the tangy flavor of the sea. Instead of shrimp, try squid, scallops, mussels or crab.

INGREDIENTS

Serves 4

4oz cellophane noodles, soaked in hot water until soft
16 cooked shrimp, peeled
1 small green bell pepper, seeded and cut into strips
½ cucumber, cut into strips
1 tomato, cut into strips
2 shallots, finely sliced
salt and black pepper
cilantro leaves, to garnish

For the dressing
1 tbsp rice vinegar
2 tbsp fish sauce
2 tbsp fresh lime juice
pinch of salt
½ tsp grated fresh ginger
1 lemongrass stalk, finely chopped
1 red chili, seeded and finely sliced
2 tbsp coarsely chopped mint
a few sprigs coarsely chopped tarragon
1 tbsp chopped chives

1 Make the dressing by combining all the ingredients in a small bowl or cup; whisk well.

2 Drain the noodles, then plunge them in a saucepan of boiling water for 1 minute. Drain, rinse under cold running water and drain again well.

3 In a large bowl, combine the noodles with the shrimp, pepper, cucumber, tomato and shallots. Lightly season with salt and pepper, then toss with the dressing.

4 Spoon the noodles onto individual plates. Garnish with a few cilantro leaves and serve at once.

NUTRITION NOTES

Per portion:
Energy	164.5Kcals/697kJ
Fat	2.9g
Saturated fat	0.79g
Cholesterol	121mg
Fiber	1.86g

COOK'S TIP
Shrimp are available ready-cooked and often shelled. To cook shrimp, boil them for 2 minutes. Allow them to cool in the cooking liquid, then gently pull off the tail shell and twist off the body.

CACHUMBAR

Cachumbar is a salad relish most commonly served with Indian curries. There are many versions; this one will leave your mouth feeling cool and fresh after a spicy meal.

INGREDIENTS

Serves 4

3 ripe tomatoes
2 chopped scallions
¼ tsp sugar
salt
3 tbsp chopped fresh cilantro

NUTRITION NOTES

Per portion:

Energy	9.5Kcals/73.5kJ
Fat	0.23g
Saturated fat	0.07g
Cholesterol	0
Fiber	0.87g

1 Remove the tough cores from the bottom of the tomatoes with a small sharp-pointed knife.

COOK'S TIP
Cachumbar also makes a fine accompaniment to fresh crab, lobster and shellfish.

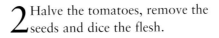

2 Halve the tomatoes, remove the seeds and dice the flesh.

3 Combine the tomatoes with the scallions, sugar, salt and chopped cilantro. Serve at room temperature.

HOT DESSERTS

When we talk of desserts and puddings we tend to imagine deliciously rich, creamy, calorie-laden treats which are well out of reach if you are following a low fat diet. However, it is very easy to create delicious, low fat desserts, full of flavor, color and appeal that will satisfy a sweet tooth any day. We include a tasty selection of hot desserts, including temptations such as Raisin and Couscous Pudding, Baked Apples in Honey and Lemon, Cinnamon and Apricot Soufflés, Blueberry and Orange Crêpe Baskets, and Blushing Pears.

STRAWBERRY AND APPLE CRISP

A high-fiber, healthier version of the classic apple crisp. Raspberries can be used instead of strawberries, either fresh or frozen.

INGREDIENTS

Serves 4
1 lb cooking apples
1¼ cups strawberries
2 tbsp sugar
½ tsp ground cinnamon
2 tbsp orange juice
yogurt, to serve

For the topping
3 tbsp plain whole-wheat flour
⅔ cup rolled oats
⅛ cup low fat margarine

1 Preheat the oven to 350°F. Peel, core and slice the apples. Halve the strawberries.

2 Toss together the apples, strawberries, sugar, cinnamon and orange juice. Pour into a 5 cup ovenproof dish, or four individual dishes.

NUTRITION NOTES

Per portion:
Energy	182.3Kcals/785kJ
Fat	4g
Saturated fat	0.73g
Cholesterol	0.5mg
Fiber	3.87g

3 Combine the flour and oats in a bowl and mix in the low fat margarine with a fork.

4 Sprinkle the topping evenly over the fruit. Bake for 40–45 minutes (20–25 minutes for individual dishes), until golden brown and bubbling. Serve warm with yogurt.

RAISIN AND COUSCOUS PUDDING

Most couscous on the market now is the pre-cooked variety, which needs only minimum cooking, but check the package instructions first to make sure. Serve hot, with yogurt or a low fat pudding.

INGREDIENTS

Serves 4

⅓ cup golden raisins
2 cups apple juice
1 cup couscous
½ tsp pumpkin pie spice

1 Lightly grease four 1 cup pudding molds or one 4 cup pudding mold. Put the raisins and apple juice in a pan.

2 Bring the apple juice to a boil, then cover the pan and let simmer gently for 2–3 minutes to plump up the fruit. Using a slotted spoon, lift out about half the fruit and put it in the bottom of the mold(s).

3 Add the couscous and pumpkin pie spice to the pan and bring back to a boil, stirring. Cover and leave over low heat for 8–10 minutes, or until the liquid has been absorbed.

NUTRITION NOTES	
Per portion:	
Energy	130.5Kcals/555kJ
Fat	0.40g
Saturated fat	0
Cholesterol	0
Fiber	0.25g

4 Spoon the couscous into the mold(s), spread it level, then cover the basin(s) tightly with foil. Put the mold(s) in a steamer over boiling water, cover and steam for about 30 minutes. Run a knife around the edges, turn the puddings out carefully and serve.

> COOK'S TIP
> As an alternative, use chopped dried apricots or pears in place of the raisins. Use unsweetened pineapple or orange juice in place of the apple juice.

CHUNKY APPLE BAKE

This filling, economical family dessert is a good way to use up slightly stale bread – any type of bread will do, but whole-wheat is richer in fiber.

INGREDIENTS

Serves 4
1 lb cooking apples
3 slices whole-wheat bread
½ cup cottage cheese
3 tbsp light brown sugar
scant 1 cup skim milk
1 tsp raw sugar

NUTRITION NOTES

Per portion:
Energy	172.5Kcals/734.7kJ
Fat	2.5g
Saturated fat	1.19g
Cholesterol	7.25mg
Fiber	2.69g

1 Preheat the oven to 425°F. Peel the apples, cut them into quarters and remove the cores.

2 Coarsely chop the apples into even-sized pieces, about ½in across.

3 Trim the crusts from the bread, then cut into ½in dice.

4 Toss together the apples, bread, cottage cheese and brown sugar.

5 Stir in the milk, then transfer the mixture into a wide ovenproof dish. Sprinkle with the raw sugar.

6 Bake the apples for about 30–35 minutes, or until golden brown and bubbling. Serve hot.

COOK'S TIP
You may need to adjust the amount of milk used, depending on the dryness of the bread; the more stale the bread, the more milk it will absorb.

BAKED APPLES IN HONEY AND LEMON

A classic mix of flavors in a healthy, traditional family dessert. Serve warm, with skim-milk pudding or low fat frozen yogurt.

INGREDIENTS

Serves 4
4 medium cooking apples
1 tbsp honey
grated rind and juice of 1 lemon
1 tbsp low fat margarine
low fat frozen yogurt, to serve

1 Preheat the oven to 350°F. Remove the cores from the apples, leaving them whole.

NUTRITION NOTES

Per portion:
Energy	61Kcals/259.5kJ
Fat	1.62g
Saturated fat	0.42g
Cholesterol	0.25mg

2 With a sharp knife, cut lines through the apple skin at intervals, then arrange the apples in an oven-proof dish.

3 Combine the honey, lemon rind, juice and low fat margarine.

4 Spoon the mixture into the apples and cover the dish with foil or a lid. Bake for 40–45 minutes, or until the apples are tender. Serve with frozen yogurt.

APPLE AND BLACK CURRANT PANCAKES

These pancakes are made with a whole-wheat batter and are filled with a delicious fruit mixture.

INGREDIENTS

Makes 10

1 cup whole-wheat flour
1¼ cups skim milk
1 egg, beaten
*1 tbsp sunflower oil, plus extra for
    greasing*
*low fat crème fraîche, to serve
    (optional)*
*toasted nuts or sesame seeds, for
    sprinkling (optional)*

For the filling
1 lb cooking apples
8oz black currants
2–3 tbsp water
2 tbsp raw sugar

1 To make the pancake batter, put the flour in a mixing bowl and make a well in the center.

2 Add a little of the milk with the egg and the oil. Beat the flour into the liquid, then gradually beat in the rest of the milk, keeping the batter smooth and free from lumps. Cover the batter and chill while you prepare the filling.

COOK'S TIP
If you wish, substitute other combinations of fruit for apples and black currants.

3 Quarter, peel and core the apples. Slice them into a pan and add the black currants and water. Cook over low heat for 10–15 minutes until the fruit is soft. Stir in enough raw sugar to sweeten.

NUTRITION NOTES	
Per portion:	
Energy	120Kcals/505kJ
Fat	3g
Saturated fat	0.5g
Cholesterol	25mg

4 Lightly grease a nonstick pan with just a smear of oil. Heat the pan, pour in about 2 tablespoons of the batter, swirl it around and cook for about 1 minute. Flip the pancake over with a spatula and cook the other side. Put on a piece of paper towel and keep hot while cooking the remaining pancakes.

5 Fill the pancakes with the apple and black currant mixture and roll them up. Serve with a dollop of crème fraîche, if using, and sprinkle with nuts or sesame seeds, if desired.

CINNAMON AND APRICOT SOUFFLÉS

Don't expect these to be difficult simply because they're soufflés – they really couldn't be easier, and, best of all, they're very low in calories.

INGREDIENTS

Serves 4

3 eggs
½ cup apricot fruit spread
finely grated rind of ½ lemon
1 tsp ground cinnamon
extra cinnamon, to decorate

NUTRITION NOTES

Per portion:

Energy	102Kcals/429kJ
Fat	4.97g
Saturated fat	1.42g
Cholesterol	176.25mg
Fiber	0

1 Preheat the oven to 375°F. Lightly grease four individual soufflé dishes and dust them lightly with flour.

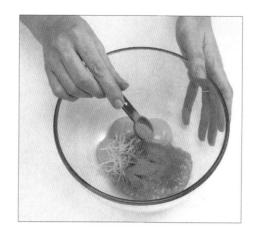

2 Separate the eggs and put the yolks in a bowl with the fruit spread, lemon rind and cinnamon.

3 Whisk hard until the mixture is thick and pale in color.

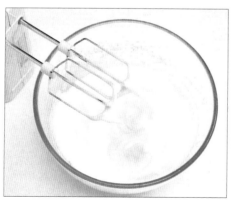

4 Place the egg whites in a clean bowl and whisk them until they are stiff enough to hold soft peaks.

5 Using a large metal spoon or spatula, fold the egg whites evenly into the yolk mixture.

6 Divide the soufflé mixture between the prepared dishes and bake for 10–15 minutes, until well risen and golden brown. Serve immediately, dusted with a little extra cinnamon.

COOK'S TIP
Puréed fresh or well-drained canned fruit can be used instead of the apricot spread, but make sure the mixture is not too wet, or the soufflés will not rise properly.

BLUEBERRY AND ORANGE CRÊPE BASKETS

Impress your guests with these pretty, fruit-filled crêpes. When blueberries are out of season, replace them with other soft fruit, such as raspberries.

INGREDIENTS

Serves 6
1¼ cups all-purpose flour
pinch of salt
2 egg whites
⅞ cup skim milk
⅔ cup orange juice
oil, for frying
low fat yogurt, to serve
For the filling
4 medium oranges
2 cups blueberries

1 Preheat the oven to 400°F. To make the crêpes, sift the flour and salt into a bowl. Make a well in the center and add the egg whites, milk and orange juice. Whisk hard, until all the liquid has been incorporated and the batter is smooth and bubbly.

2 Lightly grease a heavy or nonstick pancake pan and heat it until it is very hot. Pour in just enough batter to cover the bottom of the pan, swirling it to cover the pan evenly.

3 Cook the crêpe over medium-high heat until the crêpe has set and is golden, then turn it to cook the other side. Remove the crêpe to a piece of paper towel. Cook the remaining batter in the same way to make 6–8 crêpes.

4 Place six small ovenproof bowls or molds on a baking sheet and lay the crêpes over these. Bake them in the oven for about 10 minutes, until they are crisp and set into shape. Lift the "baskets" off the molds.

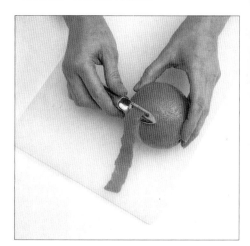

5 Pare a thin piece of orange rind from one orange and cut it into fine strips. Blanch the strips in boiling water for 30 seconds, rinse them in cold water and set them aside. Cut all the peel and white pith from the oranges.

6 Divide the oranges into segments, catching the juice, combine with the blueberries and warm them gently. Spoon the fruit into the baskets and scatter the rind over the tops. Serve with yogurt.

COOK'S TIP
Don't fill the crêpe baskets until you're ready to serve them, because they will absorb the fruit juice and begin to soften.

NUTRITION NOTES

Per portion:

Energy	157.3Kcals/668.3kJ
Fat	2.20g
Saturated fat	0.23g
Cholesterol	0.66mg
Fiber	2.87g

FILO CHIFFON PIE

Filo pastry is low in fat and is very easy to use. Keep a package in the freezer, ready to make impressive desserts like this one.

INGREDIENTS

Serves 6

1¼ lb rhubarb
1 tsp pumpkin pie spice
finely grated rind and juice of 1 orange
1 tbsp granulated sugar
1 tbsp butter
3 filo pastry sheets

1 Preheat the oven to 400°F. Wash the rhubarb, then trim and cut it into 1in pieces and put them in a bowl.

2 Add the pumpkin pie spice, orange rind and juice and sugar. Transfer the rhubarb to a 4-cup pie dish.

NUTRITION NOTES

Per portion:	
Energy	71Kcals/299kJ
Fat	2.5g
Saturated fat	1.41g
Cholesterol	5.74mg
Fiber	1.48g

3 Melt the butter and brush it over the pastry. Lift the pastry onto the pie dish, butter-side up, and crumple it up decoratively to cover the pie.

VARIATION
Other fruit can be used in this pie – just prepare depending on type.

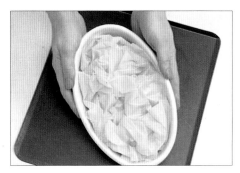

4 Put the dish on a baking sheet and bake for 20 minutes, until golden brown. Reduce the heat to 350°F and bake for another 10–15 minutes, until the rhubarb is tender.

BLUSHING PEARS

Pears poached in rosé wine and sweet spices absorb all the subtle flavors and turn a delightful soft pink color.

INGREDIENTS

Serves 6
6 firm eating pears
1¼ cups rosé wine
⅔ cup cranberry or
*   clear apple juice*
strip of thinly pared orange rind
1 cinnamon stick
4 whole cloves
1 bay leaf
5 tbsp sugar
small bay leaves, to decorate

1 Thinly peel the pears with a sharp knife or vegetable peeler, leaving the stalks attached.

2 Pour the wine and cranberry or apple juice into a large heavy saucepan. Add the orange rind, cinnamon stick, cloves, bay leaf and sugar.

3 Heat gently, stirring all the time, until the sugar has dissolved. Add the pears and stand them upright in the pan. Pour in enough cold water to barely cover them. Cover and cook gently for 20–30 minutes, or until just tender, turning and basting occasionally.

4 Using a slotted spoon, gently lift the pears out of the syrup and transfer to a serving dish.

5 Bring the syrup to a boil and boil rapidly for 10–15 minutes, or until it has reduced by half.

6 Strain the syrup and pour over the pears. Serve hot or well-chilled, decorated with small bay leaves.

NUTRITION NOTES

Per portion:
Energy	148Kcals/620kJ
Fat	0.16g
Saturated fat	0
Fiber	2.93g

COOK'S TIP
Check the pears by piercing with a skewer or sharp knife toward the end of the poaching time, because some may cook more quickly than others. Serve immediately, or allow to cool in the syrup and then chill.

COLD DESSERTS

There is such a vast range of ready-made desserts available today that there may not seem to be any point in making your own, but it is definitely well worth the effort. In no time at all, you can make and enjoy a wide variety of nutritious, delicious low fat cold desserts, such as Rhubarb and Orange Ice, Apple and Blackberry Terrine, Mandarins in Syrup, and Raspberry Vacherin.

APRICOT DELICE

A fluffy mousse base with a layer of fruit jelly on top makes this dessert doubly delicious.

INGREDIENTS

Serves 8

2 14oz cans apricots in
   natural juice
4 tbsp sugar
5 tbsp lemon juice
5 tsp powdered gelatin
15 oz low fat ready-made pudding
⅔ cup plain yogurt
1 apricot, sliced, and fresh mint sprig,
   to decorate
whipped cream, to decorate (optional)

NUTRITION NOTES

Per portion:
Energy	155Kcals/649kJ
Fat	0.63g
Saturated fat	0.33g
Fiber	0.9g

COOK'S TIP

Use low fat plain yogurt
to cut calories and fat. Add the
finely grated rind of 1 lemon
to the mixture, for extra flavor.
Peaches or pears are good
alternatives to apricots.

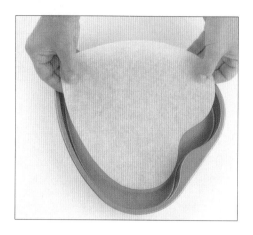

1 Line the base of a 5 cup heart-shaped or round cake tin with non-stick wax paper.

2 Drain the apricots, reserving the juice. Put the apricots in a food processor or blender fitted with a metal blade, together with the sugar and 4 tbsp of the apricot juice. Blend to a smooth purée.

3 Measure 2 tablespoons of the apricot juice into a small bowl. Add the lemon juice, then sprinkle on 2 tsp of the gelatin. Let stand for about 5 minutes, until spongy.

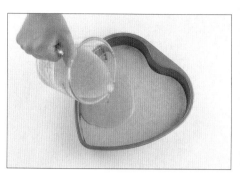

4 Stir the gelatin into half of the purée and pour into the prepared pan. Chill in the fridge for 1½ hours, or until firm.

5 Sprinkle the remaining 3 tsp of gelatin over 4 tbsp of the apricot juice. Let stand for about 5 minutes, until spongy. Mix the remaining apricot purée with the pudding, yogurt and gelatin. Pour onto the layer of set fruit purée and chill for 3 hours.

6 Dip the cake tin into hot water for a few seconds and unmold the delice onto a serving plate and peel off the lining paper. Decorate with the sliced apricot and mint sprig; for a special occasion, pipe whipped cream around the edge.

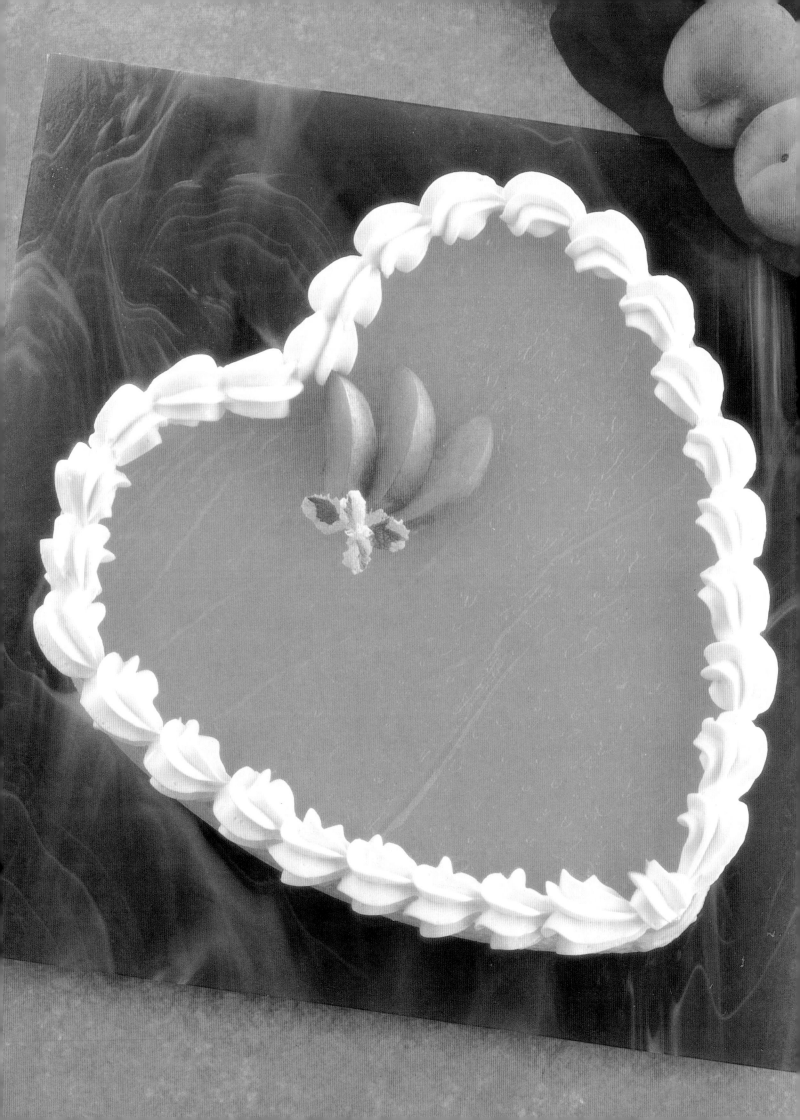

Melon, Ginger and Grapefruit

This pretty fruit combination is very light and refreshing for any summer meal.

Ingredients

Serves 4
1¼ lb diced watermelon
2 ruby or pink grapefruit
2 pieces preserved ginger in syrup
2 tbsp ginger syrup

Nutrition Notes

Per portion:
Energy	76Kcals/324.5kJ
Fat	0.42g
Saturated fat	0.125g
Cholesterol	0
Fiber	0.77g

1 Remove any seeds from the watermelon and discard. Cut the fruit into bite-size chunks. Set aside.

2 Using a small sharp knife, cut away all the peel and white pith from the grapefruit and carefully lift out the segments, catching any juice in a bowl.

3 Finely chop the ginger and put in a serving bowl with the melon cubes and grapefruit segments, also adding the juice.

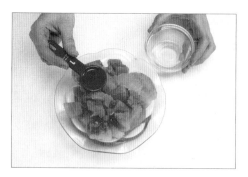

4 Spoon on the ginger syrup and toss the fruits lightly to mix evenly. Chill before serving.

> **Cook's Tip**
> Take care to toss the fruits gently – grapefruit segments will break up easily and the appearance of the dish will be spoiled.

MANGO AND GINGER CLOUDS

The sweet, perfumed flavor of ripe mango combines beautifully with ginger, and this low fat dessert makes the very most of them both.

INGREDIENTS

Serves 6
3 ripe mangoes
3 pieces preserved ginger in syrup
3 tbsp preserved ginger syrup
½ cup silken tofu
3 egg whites
6 pistachios, chopped

1 Cut the mangoes in half, remove the pits and peel. Coarsely chop the mango flesh.

2 Put the chopped mango in a food processor bowl, with the ginger, syrup and tofu. Process the mixture until smooth and spoon into a mixing bowl.

3 Put the egg whites in a bowl and whisk them until they form soft peaks. Fold them lightly into the mango mixture.

4 Spoon the mixture into wide dishes or glasses and chill before serving, sprinkled with the chopped pistachios.

NUTRITION NOTES

Per portion:	
Energy	112Kcals/472kJ
Fat	3.5g
Saturated fat	0.52g
Cholesterol	0
Fiber	2.25g

COOK'S TIP
This dessert can be served lightly frozen. If you prefer not to use ginger, omit the preserved ginger pieces and syrup and use 3 tbsp honey instead.

GOOSEBERRY CHEESE COOLER

INGREDIENTS

Serves 4

4 cups fresh or frozen
* gooseberries*
1 small orange
1 tbsp honey
1 cup low fat cottage cheese

NUTRITION NOTES

Per portion:
Energy	123Kcals/525kJ
Fat	1.29g
Saturated fat	0.69g
Cholesterol	3.25mg
Fiber	3.64g

1 Remove the ends from the gooseberries and place them in a pan. Finely grate the rind from the orange and squeeze out the juice, then add them both to the pan. Cover the pan and cook gently, stirring occasionally, until the fruit is tender.

2 Remove from the heat and stir in the honey. Purée the gooseberries with their juice in a blender or food processor until almost smooth. Cool.

3 Press the cottage cheese through a sieve until smooth. Stir half the cooled gooseberry purée into the cheese.

4 Spoon the cheese mixture into four serving glasses. Top each with gooseberry purée. Serve chilled.

COOK'S TIP
If fresh or frozen gooseberries are not available, canned ones are often packed in heavy syrup, so substitute a different fresh fruit.

MANGO AND LIME SHERBET IN LIME SHELLS

This richly flavored sherbet looks pretty served in the lime shells, but is also good served in glasses for a more traditional presentation.

INGREDIENTS

Serves 4
4 *large limes*
1 *medium-size ripe mango*
½ *tsp powdered gelatin*
2 *egg whites*
1 *tbsp sugar*
lime rind strips, to decorate

1 Cut a thick slice from the top of each of the limes, and then cut a thin slice from the bottom end so that the limes will stand upright. Squeeze out the juice, then use a small knife to remove all the white membrane from the center.

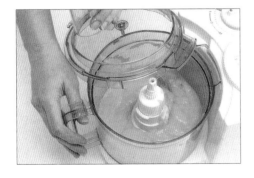

2 Halve, pit, peel and chop the mango, then purée the flesh in a blender or food processor with 2 tbsp of the lime juice. Dissolve the gelatin in 3 tbsp of lime juice and stir it into the mango mixture.

3 Whisk the egg whites until they hold soft peaks. Whisk in the sugar, then quickly fold the egg-white mixture into the mango mixture. Spoon the sherbet into the lime shells. (Any leftover sherbet that will not fit in can be frozen in small ramekins.)

COOK'S TIP
If you have any lime juice left over, it will freeze well for future use. Pour into a freezer container, seal and freeze for up to six months.

4 Wrap the shells in plastic wrap and put in the freezer until the sherbet is firm. Before serving, allow the shells to stand at room temperature for about 10 minutes; decorate them with strips of lime rind.

NUTRITION NOTES

Per portion:
Energy	50.5Kcals/215kJ
Fat	0.09g
Saturated fat	0.3g
Cholesterol	0
Fiber	1g

RHUBARB AND ORANGE WATER ICE

Pretty pink rhubarb, with sweet
oranges and honey – the perfect
sweet ice.

INGREDIENTS

Serves 4
12 ounces rhubarb
1 medium orange
1 tbsp honey
1 envelope powdered gelatin
orange slices, to decorate

COOK'S TIP
Most pink rhubarb is naturally
quite sweet, but if yours is not,
you can add a little more honey,
sugar or artificial sweetener
to taste.

1 Trim the rhubarb and slice into 1-
inch lengths. Put the pieces in a pan
without adding water.

NUTRITION NOTES

Per portion:
Energy	36Kcals/155kJ
Fat	0.12g
Saturated fat	0
Cholesterol	0
Fiber	1.9g

2 Finely grate the rind from the
orange and squeeze out the juice.
Add about half the orange juice and all
the grated rind to the rhubarb in the
pan and allow to simmer until the
rhubarb is just tender. Stir in the honey.

3 Heat the remaining orange juice
and sprinkle in the gelatin to
dissolve it. Stir into the rhubarb. Turn
the whole mixture into a rigid freezer
container and freeze it for about
2 hours, until slushy.

4 Remove the mixture from the
freezer and beat it well to break
up the ice crystals. Return to the
freezer and freeze again until firm.
Allow the ice to soften slightly at
room temperature before serving.

ICED ORANGES

The ultimate fat-free treat – these delectable orange sherbets served in fruit shells were originally sold in beach cafés in the south of France.

INGREDIENTS

Serves 8
⅔ *cup sugar*
juice of 1 lemon
14 medium oranges
8 fresh bay leaves, to decorate

NUTRITION NOTES

Per portion:	
Energy	139Kcals/593kJ
Fat	0.17g
Saturated fat	0
Cholesterol	0
Fiber	3g

COOK'S TIP
Use crumpled paper towels to keep the shells upright.

1 Put the sugar in a heavy saucepan. Add half the lemon juice, then add ½ cup water. Cook over low heat until the sugar has dissolved. Bring to a boil and boil for 2–3 minutes, until the syrup is clear.

2 Slice the tops off eight of the oranges to make "hats." Scoop out the flesh of the oranges and reserve. Freeze the empty orange shells and "hats" until needed.

3 Grate the rind of the remaining oranges and add to the syrup. Squeeze the juice from the oranges, and from the reserved flesh. There should be 3 cups. Squeeze another orange or add bought orange juice, if necessary.

4 Stir the orange juice and remaining lemon juice, with 6 tablespoons water, into the syrup. Taste, adding more lemon juice or sugar as desired. Pour the mixture into a shallow freezer container and freeze for 3 hours.

5 Turn the orange sherbet mixture into a bowl and whisk thoroughly to break up the ice crystals. Freeze for 4 hours more, until firm, but not solid.

6 Pack the mixture into the hollowed-out orange shells, mounding it up, and set the "hats" on top. Freeze the sherbet shells until ready to serve. Just before serving, make a hole with a skewer in the tops of the "hats" and push in a bay leaf, to decorate.

Apple and Blackberry Terrine

Apples and blackberries are a classic autumn combination; they really complement each other. This pretty, three-layered terrine can be frozen, so you can enjoy it at any time of year.

INGREDIENTS

Serves 6
1½ lb cooking or eating apples
1¼ cups sweet cider
1 tbsp honey
1 tsp vanilla extract
7oz fresh or thawed, frozen
   blackberries
1 envelope powdered gelatin
2 egg whites
apple slices and blackberries, to
   decorate

NUTRITION NOTES

Per portion:
Energy	72Kcals/306kJ
Fat	0.13g
Saturated fat	0
Cholesterol	0
Fiber	2.1g

COOK'S TIP

For a quicker version of the terrine, the mixture can be set without layering. Purée the apples and blackberries together, stir the dissolved gelatin and whisked egg whites into the mixture, transfer the whole thing to the pan and let the mixture set.

1 Peel, core and chop the apples and place them in a saucepan, with half the cider. Bring the cider to a boil, and then cover the pan and let the apples simmer gently over medium heat until tender.

2 Transfer the apples to a blender or food processor and process to a smooth purée. Stir in the honey and vanilla. Add half the blackberries to half the apple purée, and then process the mixture again until smooth. Strain.

3 Heat the remaining cider until it is almost boiling, then sprinkle on the powdered gelatin and stir until the gelatin has completely dissolved. Add half the gelatin and cider liquid to the apple purée and half to the blackberry purée.

4 Allow the purées to cool until almost set. Whisk the egg whites until they are stiff, then quickly fold them into the apple purée. Remove half the purée to another bowl. Stir the remaining whole blackberries into half the apple purée, and then turn this into a 8-cup loaf pan.

5 Top with the blackberry purée and spread it evenly. Finally, add a layer of the apple purée and smooth it evenly. To make sure the layers remain clearly separated, you can freeze each one until firm before adding the next.

6 Freeze until firm. To serve, allow to stand at room temperature for about 20 minutes to soften, then serve in thick slices, decorated with apples and blackberries.

QUICK APRICOT WHIP

Serves 4

1 14oz can apricot halves in juice
1 tbsp Grand Marnier or brandy
¾ cup low fat yogurt
2 tsp flaked almonds

NUTRITION NOTES

Per portion:

Energy	114Kcals/480kJ
Fat	4.6g
Saturated fat	0.57g
Cholesterol	0
Fiber	1.45g

1 Drain the juice from the apricots and place the fruit and liqueur in a blender or food processor.

2 Process the apricots until they are completely smooth.

3 Put alternate spoonfuls of the fruit purée and yogurt into four tall glasses or glass dishes, swirling them together slightly to give a marbled effect.

4 Lightly toast the almonds until they are golden-brown. Let them cool slightly and then sprinkle them on top of the desserts.

> **COOK'S TIP**
> If you prefer to omit the liqueur, add a little of the fruit juice from the can.

MANDARINS IN SYRUP

Mandarins, tangerines, clementines, mineolas: any of these lovely citrus fruits are suitable for this recipe.

INGREDIENTS

Serves 4
10 mandarin oranges
1 tbsp confectioners' sugar
2 tsp orange-flower water
1 tbsp chopped pistachios

1 Thinly pare a little of the rind from one mandarin and cut it into fine shreds for decoration. Squeeze the juice from two mandarins and set aside.

2 Peel the remaining fruit, removing as much of the white pith as possible. Arrange the peeled whole fruit in a wide dish.

3 Mix the mandarin juice, sugar and orange-flower water and pour it over the fruit. Cover the dish and chill for at least an hour.

4 Blanch the shreds of mandarin rind in boiling water for 30 seconds. Drain, allow to cool and then sprinkle them over the mandarins, with the pistachios, to serve.

NUTRITION NOTES

Per portion:
Energy	53.25Kcals/223.5kJ
Fat	2.07g
Saturated fat	0.28g
Cholesterol	0
Fiber	0.38g

COOK'S TIP
Mandarin oranges look very attractive if you leave them whole, but you may prefer to separate the segments.

CRUNCHY FRUIT LAYER

INGREDIENTS

Serves 2

1 peach or nectarine
1 cup crunchy granola with nuts
⅔ cup low fat plain yogurt
1 tbsp jam
1 tbsp fruit juice

NUTRITION NOTES

Per portion:
Energy	240Kcals/1005kJ
Fat	3g
Saturated fat	1g
Cholesterol	3mg

1 Remove the pit from the peach or nectarine and cut the fruit into bite-size pieces with a sharp knife.

2 Divide the chopped fruit between two tall glasses, reserving a few pieces for decoration.

3 Sprinkle the granola over the fruit in an even layer, then top with the low fat yogurt.

4 Stir the jam and the fruit juice together in a cup, then drizzle the mixture over the yogurt. Decorate with the reserved peach or nectarine pieces and serve immediately.

RASPBERRY GRANOLA LAYER

As well as being a delicious, low fat, high-fiber dessert, this recipe can also be served for a quick, healthy breakfast.

───── **INGREDIENTS** ─────

Serves 4

2¼ cups fresh or frozen and thawed raspberries
1 cup low fat plain yogurt
½ cup Swiss-style granola

1 Reserve four raspberries for decoration, then spoon a few raspberries into each of four stemmed glasses or glass dishes.

2 Top the raspberries with a spoonful of yogurt in each glass.

> COOK'S TIP
> This recipe can be made in advance and stored in the fridge for several hours, or overnight if you're serving it for breakfast.

3 Sprinkle a layer of granola mixture over the yogurt.

4 Repeat with the remaining raspberries and other ingredients, finishing with granola. Top each dish with a whole raspberry.

───── **NUTRITION NOTES** ─────

Per portion:

Energy	114Kcals/483kJ
Fat	1.7g
Saturated fat	0.48g
Cholesterol	2.25mg
Fiber	2.6g

YOGURT SUNDAES WITH PASSIONFRUIT

Here is a sundae you can enjoy every day! The frozen yogurt has less fat and fewer calories than traditional ice cream, and the fruits provide vitamins A and C.

INGREDIENTS

Serves 4
12oz strawberries, hulled
 and halved
2 passionfruit, halved
2 tsp confectioners' sugar
2 ripe peaches, pitted and chopped
8 scoops (about 12oz) vanilla or
 strawberry frozen yogurt

COOK'S TIP
Choose reduced-fat or virtually fat-free frozen yogurt or ice cream, to cut the calories and fat.

1 Purée half the strawberries. Scoop out the passionfruit pulp and add it to the sauce. Sweeten, if necessary.

NUTRITION NOTES

Per portion:	
Energy	135Kcals/560kJ
Fat	1g
Saturated fat	0.5g
Cholesterol	3.5mg

2 Spoon half the remaining strawberries and half the chopped peaches into four tall sundae glasses. Top each dessert with a scoop of frozen yogurt. Set aside a few choice pieces of fruit for decoration, and use the rest to make another layer on the top of each sundae. Top each sundae with a final scoop of frozen yogurt.

3 Top with the passionfruit sauce and decorate the sundaes with the remaining strawberries and pieces of peach. Serve immediately.

FRUIT FONDUE WITH HAZELNUT DIP

INGREDIENTS

Serves 2
selection of fresh fruit for dipping, such
 as clementines, figs, apricots, grapes,
 nectarines and plums
½ cup reduced fat cream cheese
1¼ cup low fat vanilla yogurt
1 tsp vanilla extract
1 tsp sugar

NUTRITION NOTES

Per portion (dip only):	
Energy	170Kcals/714kJ
Fat	4g
Saturated fat	2.5g
Cholesterol	6.5mg

1 First prepare the fruit. Peel and segment the clementines, removing as much of the white pith as possible. Quarter the fresh figs and apricots, wash the grapes and slice the nectarines and plums.

2 Beat the cream cheese with the yogurt, vanilla extract and sugar in a bowl. Spoon the mixture into a glass serving dish set on a platter or into small dishes on individual plates.

3 Arrange the prepared fruits around the dip and serve immediately.

PINEAPPLE, ALLSPICE AND LIME

Fresh pineapple is easy to prepare and always looks very festive, so this dish is perfect for easy entertaining.

INGREDIENTS

Serves 4
1 ripe medium pineapple
1 lime
1 tbsp dark brown sugar
1 tsp ground allspice

1 Cut the pineapple lengthwise into quarters and remove the core.

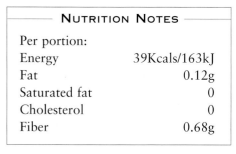

2 Loosen the fruit by sliding a knife between it and the skin. Cut the pineapple flesh into thick slices.

3 Remove a few shreds of rind from the lime and set aside, then squeeze out the juice.

4 Sprinkle the pineapple with the lime juice and rind, brown sugar and all-spice. Serve immediately, or chill for up to 1 hour.

NUTRITION NOTES	
Per portion:	
Energy	39Kcals/163kJ
Fat	0.12g
Saturated fat	0
Cholesterol	0
Fiber	0.68g

Papaya Skewers with Passionfruit

Tropical fruits, full of natural sweetness, make a simple dessert.

Ingredients

Serves 6

3 ripe papayas
10 small passionfruit or kiwi fruit
2 tbsp lime juice
2 tbsp confectioners' sugar
2 tbsp white rum
toasted coconut, to garnish (optional)

Nutrition Notes

Per portion:

Energy	83Kcals/351kJ
Fat	0.27g
Saturated fat	0
Cholesterol	0
Fiber	2.8g

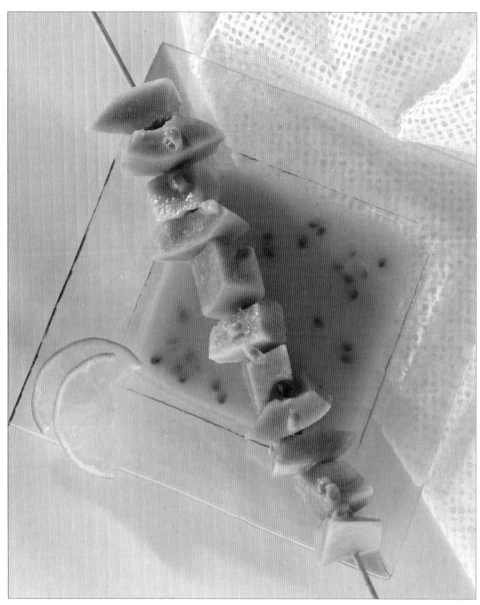

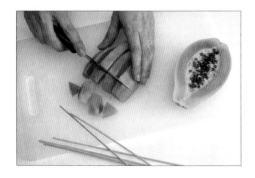

1 Cut the papayas in half and scoop out the seeds. Peel and cut the flesh into even-size chunks. Thread the chunks onto six bamboo skewers.

2 Halve eight of the passionfruit or kiwi fruit and scoop out the insides. Purée for a few seconds in a blender or food processor.

3 Press the passionfruit or kiwi fruit pulp through a strainer and discard the seeds. Add the lime juice, confectioners' sugar and white rum, then stir the sauce well until the sugar has dissolved.

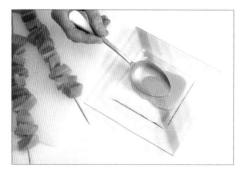

4 Spoon a little of the sauce onto six serving plates. Place the skewers on top. Scoop the flesh from the remaining passionfruit or kiwi fruit and spoon it over. Sprinkle with a little toasted coconut, if desired, and serve.

RASPBERRY VACHERIN

Meringue rounds filled with orange-flavored low fat cream cheese and fresh raspberries make this a perfect dinner party dessert.

Serves 6
3 egg whites
¾ cup superfine sugar
1 tsp chopped almonds
confectioners' sugar, for dusting
raspberry leaves, to decorate (optional)

For the filling
¾ cup low fat cream cheese
1–2 tbsp honey
1–2 tbsp Cointreau
½ cup low fat ricotta
  or farmer's cheese
8oz raspberries

NUTRITION NOTES

Per portion:
Energy	197Kcals/837.5kJ
Fat	1.02g
Saturated fat	0.36g
Cholesterol	1.67mg
Fiber	1g

COOK'S TIP
When making the meringue, whisk the egg whites until they are so stiff that you can turn the bowl upside-down without their falling out.

1 Preheat the oven to 275°F. Draw an 8in circle on two pieces of non-stick parchment paper. Turn the paper over so the marking is on the under-side and use it to line two heavy baking sheets.

2 Whisk the egg whites in a clean bowl until very stiff, then gradually whisk in the superfine sugar to make a stiff meringue mixture.

3 Spoon the mixture onto the circles on the prepared baking sheets, spreading the meringue evenly to the edges. Sprinkle one meringue round with the chopped almonds.

4 Bake for 1½–2 hours or until crisp and dry, then carefully lift the meringue rounds off the baking sheets. Peel away the paper and cool the meringues on a wire rack.

5 To make the filling, cream the soft cheese with the honey and liqueur in a bowl. Gradually fold in the ricotta cheese and the raspberries, reserving three berries for decoration.

6 Place the plain meringue round on a board, spread with the filling and top with the nut-covered round. Dust with the confectioners' sugar, transfer to a serving plate and decorate with the reserved raspberries and a sprig of raspberry leaves, if desired.

COOL GREEN FRUIT SALAD

A sophisticated, simple fruit salad for any time of year.

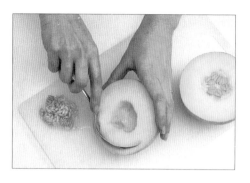

INGREDIENTS

Serves 6
3 cantaloupes
4oz green seedless grapes
2 kiwi fruit
1 star fruit
1 green-skinned eating apple
1 lime
3/4 cup sparkling grape juice

NUTRITION NOTES

Per portion:

Energy	67Kcals/285kJ
Fat	0.27g
Saturated fat	0
Cholesterol	0
Fiber	1.22g

1 Cut the melons in half and scoop out the seeds. Keeping the shells intact, scoop out the fruit with a melon baller, or scoop it out with a spoon and cut into bite-size cubes. Set aside the melon shells.

> COOK'S TIP
> If you're serving this dessert on a hot summer day, serve the filled melon shells nestling on a platter of crushed ice to keep them beautifully cool.

2 Remove any stems from the grapes and, if they are large, cut them in half. Peel and chop the kiwi fruit. Thinly slice the star fruit. Core and thinly slice the apple and place the slices in a bowl with the melon, grapes, kiwi fruit and star fruit.

3 Thinly pare the rind from the lime and cut it into fine strips. Blanch the strips in boiling water for 30 seconds, then drain them and rinse in cold water. Squeeze the juice from the lime and toss it into the fruit. Mix gently.

4 Spoon the prepared fruit into the melon shells and chill in the fridge until required. Just before serving, spoon the sparkling grape juice over the fruit and sprinkle it with the blanched lime rind.

THREE FRUIT COMPOTES

INGREDIENTS

Each Compote Serves 1

ORANGE AND PRUNE COMPOTE
1 orange
2oz pitted prunes
5 tbsp orange juice

PEAR AND KIWI FRUIT COMPOTE
1 ripe pear
1 kiwi fruit
4 tbsp apple or pineapple juice

GRAPEFRUIT AND STRAWBERRY COMPOTE
1 ruby grapefruit
4oz strawberries
4 tbsp orange juice

To serve
*low fat plain yogurt and toasted
  hazelnuts*

NUTRITION NOTES

Per portion (minus topping):

Orange and Prune

Energy	155Kcals/650kJ
Fat	0.5g
Saturated fat	0
Cholesterol	0

Pear and Kiwi Fruit

Energy	100Kcals/405kJ
Fat	0.5g
Saturated fat	0
Cholesterol	0

Grapefruit and Strawberry

Energy	110Kcals/465kJ
Fat	0.5g
Saturated fat	0
Cholesterol	0

COOK'S TIP
Choose fresh-squeezed fruit juices
or make your own using a juicer
or food processor.

3 For the grapefruit and strawberry compote, divide the grapefruit into segments and halve the strawberries.

4 Put your selected fruits together in a bowl and pour on the fruit juice.

5 Serve the chosen fruit compote topped with a spoonful of low fat plain yogurt and a sprinkling of chopped toasted hazelnuts, to decorate.

1 For the orange and prune compote, divide the orange into segments and place them in a bowl with the prunes.

2 For the pear and kiwi fruit compote, peel the pear and cut it into wedges, and peel and slice the kiwi fruit.

Prune and Orange Pots

This simple dessert can be made in minutes from supplies at hand. Serve immediately or, for the best result, chill it for about half an hour before serving.

INGREDIENTS

Serves 4
1½ cups dried prunes
⅔ cup orange juice
1 cup low fat plain yogurt
shreds of orange rind,
* to decorate*

NUTRITION NOTES

Per portion:
Energy	112Kcals/474kJ
Fat	0.62g
Saturated fat	0.34g
Cholesterol	2.25mg
Fiber	2.8g

1 Remove the pits from the prunes and coarsely chop them. Place them in a pan with the orange juice.

2 Bring the juice to a boil, stirring. Reduce the heat, cover and let simmer for 5 minutes, until the prunes are tender and the liquid has reduced by about half.

3 Remove from the heat, allow to cool slightly and then beat well with a wooden spoon, until the fruit breaks down to a rough purée.

> COOK'S TIP
> This dessert can also be made with other dried fruit, such as apricots or peaches. For a special occasion, add a dash of brandy or Cointreau with the yogurt.

4 Transfer the purée to a bowl. Stir in the low fat yogurt, swirling the yogurt and fruit purée together lightly to give the dessert an attractive marbled effect.

5 Spoon the mixture into individual dishes or stemmed glasses, smoothing the tops.

6 Top each pot with a few shreds of orange rind, to decorate. Chill before serving.

TROPICAL YOGURT RING

An impressive, light and colorful tropical dessert with a truly fruity flavor.

INGREDIENTS

Serves 6
For the yogurt ring
¾ cup tropical fruit juice
1 envelope powdered gelatin
3 egg whites
1 cup low fat plain yogurt
finely grated rind of 1 lime

For the filling
1 mango
2 kiwi fruit
½ cup raspberries
juice of 1 lime

1 Place the tropical fruit juice in a small pan and sprinkle on the powdered gelatin. Heat gently until the gelatin has dissolved.

2 Whisk the egg whites in a clean, dry bowl until they hold soft peaks. Continue whisking hard, while gradually adding the yogurt and lime rind.

3 Continue whisking hard and pour in the hot gelatin and the egg white and yogurt mixture in a steady stream, until everything is smooth and evenly mixed.

4 Quickly pour the mixture into a 6 cup ring mold. Chill the mold in the fridge until set. The mixture will separate into two layers.

5 Halve, pit, peel and dice the mango. Peel and slice the kiwi fruit. Pick over the raspberries carefully. Toss all the fruits together and stir in the lime juice.

6 Run a knife around the edge of the ring to loosen the mixture. Dip the mold quickly into cold water and then turn the chilled yogurt mold out onto a serving plate. Spoon all the prepared fruit into the center of the ring and serve immediately.

NUTRITION NOTES

Per portion:	
Energy	83.5Kcals/355kJ
Fat	0.67g
Saturated fat	0.27g
Cholesterol	2.16mg
Fiber	1.77g

COOK'S TIP
Any mixture of fruit works in this recipe, depending on the season. In summer try using apple juice in the ring mixture and fill it with luscious, red summer fruits.

STRAWBERRY ROSE-PETAL PASHKA

This lighter version of a traditional Russian dessert is ideal for dinner parties – make it a day or two in advance for best results.

INGREDIENTS

Serves 4

1½ *cups cottage cheese*
¾ *cup low fat plain yogurt*
2 *tbsp honey*
½ *tsp rose-water*
10oz *strawberries*
handful of scented pink rose petals,
   to decorate

NUTRITION NOTES

Per portion:

Energy	150.5Kcals/634kJ
Fat	3.83g
Saturated fat	2.32g
Cholesterol	0.13mg
Fiber	0.75g

COOK'S TIP
The flowerpot shape is traditional for pashka, but you could make it in any shape – the small porcelain heart-shaped molds with draining holes usually used for *coeurs à la crème* make a pretty alternative.

1 Drain any liquid from the cottage cheese and put the cheese in a strainer. Use a wooden spoon to rub it through the strainer into a bowl.

2 Stir the yogurt, honey and rose-water into the cheese.

3 Coarsely chop about half the strawberries and stir them into the cheese mixture.

4 Line a new, clean flowerpot or a strainer with cheesecloth and put the cheese mixture in it. Let drain over a bowl for several hours, or overnight.

5 Invert the flowerpot or strainer onto a serving plate, turn out the pashka and remove the cheesecloth.

6 Decorate the pashka with strawberries and rose petals. Serve chilled.

CAKES AND BARS

We tend to think of cakes and bars as being out of
bounds for those following a low fat diet, but you
will be pleased to learn that this is not the case at all. There
are many ways of creating delicious cakes and treats without
the need for high fat ingredients, and all the foods in this
chapter, both sweet and savory, are low in fat. Choose from
tempting recipes for such delights as Tia Maria Sponge Cake,
Coffee Sponge Drops, Brown Sugar Meringues, and
Chocolate and Banana Brownies.

IRISH WHISKEY CAKE

This moist rich fruit cake is drizzled with whiskey as soon as it comes out of the oven.

INGREDIENTS

Serves 12
⅔ cup candied cherries
1 cup dark brown sugar
⅔ cup golden raisins
⅔ cup dark raisins
½ cup currants
1¼ cups cold tea
2½ cups self-rising
   flour, sifted
1 egg
3 tbsp Irish whiskey

COOK'S TIP
If time is short, use hot tea and soak the fruit for just 2 hours.

1 Mix the cherries, sugar, dried fruit and tea in a large bowl. Allow to soak overnight until all the tea has been absorbed into the fruit.

NUTRITION NOTES

Per portion:
Energy	265Kcals/1115kJ
Fat	0.88g
Saturated fat	0.25g
Cholesterol	16mg
Fiber	1.48g

2 Preheat the oven to 350°F. Grease and line a 2¼ lb loaf pan. Add the flour, then the egg to the fruit mixture and beat thoroughly until well mixed.

3 Pour the mixture into the prepared pan and bake for 1½ hours or until a skewer inserted into the center of the cake comes out clean.

4 Prick the top of the cake with a skewer and drizzle on the whiskey while the cake is still hot. Allow to stand for about 5 minutes, then remove from the pan and cool on a wire rack.

ANGEL CAKE

This cake makes a delicious light dessert, served on its own or with fresh fruit.

Serves 10
¹/₃ cup cornstarch
¹/₃ cup all-purpose flour
8 egg whites
1 cup superfine sugar, plus extra for
  sprinkling
1 tsp vanilla extract
confectioners' sugar, for dusting

1 Preheat the oven to 350°F. Sift the flour and the cornstarch onto a sheet of wax paper.

2 Whisk the egg whites in a large, clean, dry bowl until very stiff, then gradually add the sugar and vanilla extract, whisking until the mixture is thick and glossy.

3 Gently fold in the flour mixture with a large metal spoon. Spoon into an ungreased 10-inch angel cake pan, smooth the surface and bake for about 45–50 minutes, or until the cake springs back when lightly pressed.

COOK'S TIP
Low fat cream cheese and fresh fruit are the ideal complement to this cake.

4 Sprinkle a piece of wax paper with sugar and set an egg cup in the center. Invert the cake pan over the paper, balancing it carefully on the egg cup. When cold, the cake will drop out of the tin. Transfer it to a plate, decorate, if desired, then dust with confectioners' sugar and serve.

NUTRITION NOTES	
Per portion:	
Energy	139Kcals/582kJ
Fat	0.08g
Saturated fat	0.01g
Cholesterol	0
Fiber	0.13g

TIA MARIA SPONGE CAKE

A feather-light coffee sponge with a creamy liqueur-flavored filling.

INGREDIENTS

Serves 8
¾ cup all-purpose flour
2 tbsp instant coffee powder
3 eggs
½ cup superfine sugar
coffee beans, to decorate (optional)

For the filling
¾ cup low fat cream cheese
1 tbsp honey
1 tbsp Tia Maria liqueur
¼ cup preserved ginger,
coarsely chopped

For the icing
1¾ cups confectioners' sugar, sifted
2 tsp coffee extract
1 tbsp water
1 tsp reduced-fat cocoa powder

NUTRITION NOTES

Per portion:	
Energy	226Kcals/951kJ
Fat	3.14g
Saturated fat	1.17g
Cholesterol	75.03mg
Fiber	0.64g

COOK'S TIP
When folding in the flour mixture, take care not to beat out all the air, as it helps the cake to rise.

1 Preheat the oven to 375°F. Grease and line an 8-inch deep round cake pan. Sift the flour and coffee powder together onto a sheet of wax paper.

2 Whisk the eggs and sugar in a bowl with a hand-held electric whisk until thick and mousse-like. (When the whisk is lifted, a trail should remain on the surface of the mixture for at least 15 seconds.)

3 Gently fold in the flour mixture with a rubber spatula. Turn the mixture into the prepared pan. Bake for 30–35 minutes or until it springs back when lightly pressed. Turn onto a wire rack to cool completely.

4 To make the filling, mix the soft cheese with the honey in a bowl. Beat until smooth, then stir in the Tia Maria and chopped stem ginger.

5 Split the cake in half horizontally and sandwich the two halves together with the Tia Maria filling.

6 Make the icing. In a bowl, mix the confectioners' sugar and coffee extract with enough water to make a consistency that will coat the back of a wooden spoon. Pour three-quarters of the icing over the cake, spreading it evenly to the edges. Stir the cocoa into the remaining icing until smooth. Spoon into a pastry bag fitted with a writing nozzle and pipe the mocha icing over the coffee icing. Decorate with coffee beans, if desired.

CHOCOLATE AND ORANGE ANGEL CAKE

This light-as-air sponge with its fluffy icing is virtually fat free, yet tastes heavenly.

INGREDIENTS

Serves 10
¼ cup all-purpose flour
2 tbsp reduced-fat
   cocoa powder
2 tbsp cornstarch
pinch of salt
5 egg whites
½ tsp cream of tartar
scant ½ cup superfine sugar
blanched and shredded rind of
   1 orange, to decorate

For the icing
1 cup superfine sugar
1 egg white

NUTRITION NOTES

Per portion:
Energy	53Kcals/644kJ
Fat	0.27g
Saturated fat	0.13g
Fiber	0.25g

COOK'S TIP
Make sure you do not overbeat the egg whites. They should not be stiff but should form soft peaks, so that the air bubbles can expand during cooking and help the cake to rise.

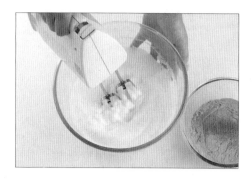

1 Preheat the oven to 350°F. Sift the flour, cocoa powder, cornstarch and salt together three times. Beat the egg whites in a large clean, dry bowl until foamy. Add the cream of tartar, then whisk until soft peaks form.

2 Add the sugar to the egg whites a spoonful at a time, whisking after each addition. Sift a third of the flour and cocoa mixture over the meringue and gently fold in. Repeat, sifting and folding in the flour and cocoa mixture two more times.

3 Spoon the mixture into a nonstick 8-inch ring mold and level the top. Bake in the oven for 35 minutes or until springy when pressed lightly. Turn upside-down onto a wire rack and allow to cool in the pan. Carefully ease out of the pan.

4 For the icing, put the sugar in a pan with 5 tablespoons cold water. Stir over low heat until dissolved. Boil until the syrup reaches a temperature of 240°F on a sugar thermometer, or until a drop of the syrup makes a soft ball when dropped into a cup of cold water. Remove from the heat.

5 Whisk the egg white until stiff. Add the syrup in a thin stream, whisking constantly. Continue to whisk until the mixture is very thick and fluffy.

6 Spread the icing over the top and sides of the cooled cake. Sprinkle the orange rind over the top of the cake and serve.

CINNAMON APPLE GÂTEAU

Make this lovely cake for an autumn celebration.

INGREDIENTS

Serves 8
3 eggs
¹/₂ cup sugar
³/₄ cup all-purpose flour
1 tsp ground cinnamon

For the filling and topping
4 large eating apples
4 tbsp honey
1 tbsp water
¹/₂ cup golden raisins
¹/₂ tsp ground cinnamon
1¹/₂ cups low fat cream cheese
4 tbsp reduced fat ricotta cheese
2 tsp lemon juice
3 tbsp apricot glaze
mint sprig, to decorate

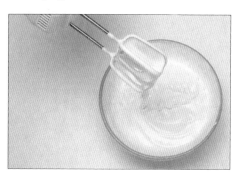

1 Preheat the oven to 375°F. Grease and line a 9 in layer cake pan. Place the eggs and sugar in a bowl and beat with a hand-held electric whisk until thick and mousse-like. (When the whisk is lifted, a trail should remain on the surface of the mixture for at least 15 seconds.)

NUTRITION NOTES

Per portion:
Energy	244Kcals/1023kJ
Fat	4.05g
Saturated fat	1.71g
Cholesterol	77.95mg
Fiber	1.50g

2 Sift the flour and cinnamon over the egg mixture and fold in with a rubber spatula. Pour into the prepared pan and bake for 25–30 minutes or until the cake springs back when lightly pressed. Turn the cake onto a wire rack to cool.

3 To make the filling, peel, core and slice three of the apples and put them in a saucepan. Add 2 tbsp of the honey and the water. Cover and cook over gentle heat for about 10 minutes. Add the raisins and cinnamon, stir well, replace the lid and let cool.

4 Put the cream cheese in a bowl with the remaining honey, the ricotta cheese and half the lemon juice. Beat until the mixture is smooth.

5 Halve the cake horizontally, place the bottom half on a board and drizzle over any liquid from the apples. Spread with two-thirds of the cheese mixture, then top with the apple filling. Fit the top of the cake in place.

6 Swirl the remaining cheese mixture over the top of the cake. Core and slice the remaining apple, sprinkle with lemon juice and use to decorate the edge of the cake. Brush the apple with the apricot glaze and place mint sprigs on top, to decorate.

COOK'S TIP
Apricot glaze is useful for brushing over any kind of fresh fruit topping or filling. Place a few spoonfuls of apricot jam in a small pan along with a squeeze of lemon juice. Heat the jam, stirring until it is melted and runny. Pour the melted jam into a wire strainer set over a bowl. Stir the jam with a wooden spoon to help it go through. Return the strained jam to the pan. Keep the glaze warm until needed.

SNOWBALLS

These light and airy little mouthfuls make an excellent accompaniment to low-fat yogurt or ice cream.

INGREDIENTS

Makes about 20
2 egg whites
½ cup superfine sugar
1 tbsp cornstarch, sifted
1 tsp white wine vinegar
¼ tsp vanilla extract

1 Preheat the oven to 300°F. Line a baking sheet with nonstick parchment paper. Whisk the egg whites in a clean, dry bowl until very stiff, using an electric whisk.

2 Add the sugar, whisking until the meringue is very stiff. Whisk in the cornstarch, vinegar and vanilla extract.

3 Drop teaspoonfuls of the mixture onto the baking sheets, shaping them into mounds, and bake for 30 minutes, until crisp.

4 Remove from the oven and allow to cool on the baking sheet. When the snowballs are cold, remove them from the baking paper with a spatula.

NUTRITION NOTES

Per portion:
Energy	29Kcals/24kJ
Fat	0.01g
Saturated fat	0
Cholesterol	0

MUSCOVADO MERINGUES

These light brown meringues are extremely low in fat and are delicious served on their own or sandwiched together with a fresh fruit and soft cheese filling.

INGREDIENTS

Makes about 20
⅔ cup light brown sugar
2 egg whites
1 tsp finely chopped walnuts

NUTRITION NOTES

Per portion:
Energy	30Kcals/124kJ
Fat	0.34g
Saturated fat	0.04g
Cholesterol	0
Fiber	0.02g

1 Preheat the oven to 325°F. Line two baking sheets with nonstick parchment paper. Press the sugar through a metal strainer into a bowl.

2 Whisk the egg whites in a clean, dry bowl until very stiff and dry, then whisk in the sugar, about 1 tbsp at a time, until the meringue is very thick and glossy.

3 Spoon small mounds of the mixture onto the prepared baking sheets.

4 Sprinkle the meringues with the chopped walnuts. Bake for 30 minutes. Cool for 5 minutes on the baking sheets, then let cool on a wire rack.

COOK'S TIP
For a sophisticated filling, mix ½ cup low-fat cream cheese with 1 tbsp confectioners' sugar. Chop 2 slices of fresh pineapple and add to the mixture. Use to sandwich the meringues together in pairs.

LEMON SPONGE FINGERS

These tangy, light sponge fingers are virtually fat-free and perfect to serve either as an accompaniment to low-fat desserts, or to serve with coffee.

INGREDIENTS

Makes about 20
2 eggs
½ cup superfine sugar
grated rind of 1 lemon
½ cup all-purpose flour, sifted
sugar, for sprinkling

NUTRITION NOTES	
Per portion:	
Energy	33Kcals/137kJ
Fat	0.57g
Saturated fat	0.16g
Cholesterol	19.30mg
Fiber	0.08g

1 Preheat the oven to 375°F. Line two baking sheets with nonstick parchment paper.

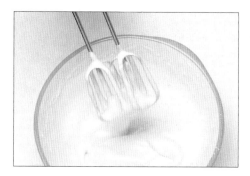

2 Whisk the eggs, sugar and lemon rind together with an electric whisk until the mixture is thick and mousse-like and leaves a thick trail on the surface for at least 15 seconds.

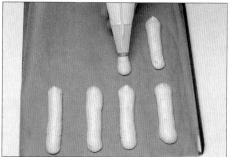

3 Carefully fold in the flour with a large rubber spatula. Place the mixture in a large pastry bag fitted with a ½in plain nozzle and pipe into finger lengths on the baking sheets.

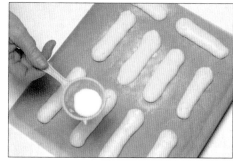

4 Dust with sugar and bake for 6–8 minutes until golden brown.

VARIATION
To make Spice Fingers, omit the lemon rind and fold in 1 tsp pumpkin pie spice with the flour.

APRICOT SPONGE BARS

These fingers are delicious at tea time – the apricots keep them moist for several days.

INGREDIENTS

Makes 18
2 cups self-rising flour
¹/₂ cup light brown sugar
¹/₂ cup semolina
1 cup dried apricots,
  chopped
2 tbsp honey
2 tbsp malt extract
2 eggs
4 tbsp skim milk
4 tbsp sunflower oil
a few drops of almond extract
2 tbsp flaked almonds

1 Preheat the oven to 325°F. Lightly grease and then line an 7 x 11 in baking pan.

2 Sift the flour into a bowl and mix in the sugar, semolina and apricots. Make a well in the center and add the honey, malt extract, eggs, milk, oil and almond extract. Mix the ingredients together thoroughly until smooth.

3 Spoon the mixture into the pan, spreading it to the edges, then sprinkle over the flaked almonds.

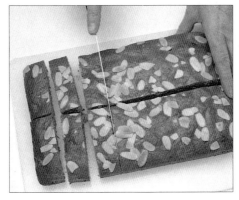

4 Bake for 30–35 minutes, or until the center springs back when lightly pressed. Remove from the pan and turn out on a wire rack to cool. Cut into 18 slices, using a sharp knife.

COOK'S TIP
Malt extract is not widely available; look for it in health food stores. A possible substitute would be maple extract, but the flavor is different.

NUTRITION NOTES

Per portion:

Energy	153Kcals/641kJ
Fat	4.56g
Saturated Fat	0.61g
Cholesterol	21.5mg
Fiber	1.27g

COFFEE SPONGE DROPS

These are delicious on their own, but taste even better with a filling made by mixing low fat cream cheese with drained and chopped preserved ginger.

INGREDIENTS

Makes 12
½ cup all-purpose flour
1 tbsp instant
  coffee powder
2 eggs
6 tbsp superfine sugar

For the filling
½ cup low fat cream cheese
¼ cup chopped preserved ginger

COOK'S TIP
As an alternative to preserved ginger in the filling, try walnuts.

NUTRITION NOTES

Per portion:
Energy	69Kcals/290kJ
Fat	1.36g
Saturated fat	0.50g
Cholesterol	33.33mg
Fiber	0.29g

1 Preheat the oven to 375°F. Line two baking sheets with nonstick parchment paper. Make the filling by beating together the cream cheese and preserved ginger. Chill until needed. Sift the flour and instant coffee powder together.

2 Combine the eggs and superfine sugar in a bowl. Beat with a hand-held electric whisk until thick and mousse-like. (When the whisk is lifted, a trail should remain on the surface of the mixture for at least 15 seconds.)

3 Carefully add the sifted flour and coffee mixture and gently fold in with a rubber spatula, being careful not to knock out any air.

4 Spoon the mixture into a pastry bag fitted with a ½in plain nozzle. Pipe 1½in rounds on the baking sheets. Bake for 12 minutes. Cool on a wire rack, then sandwich together with the filling.

CHOCOLATE AND BANANA BROWNIES

Nuts traditionally give brownies their chewy texture. Here oat bran is used instead, creating a low fat, moist, denser, yet healthy alternative.

INGREDIENTS

Serves 9

5 tbsp cocoa powder
1 tbsp sugar
5 tbsp skim milk
3 large bananas, mashed
1 cup light brown sugar
1 tsp vanilla extract
5 egg whites
¾ cup self-rising flour
¾ cup oat bran
1 tbsp confectioners' sugar

NUTRITION NOTES

Per portion:
Energy	152Kcals/637kJ
Fat	2.15g
Saturated fat	0.91g
Fiber	1.89g

COOK'S TIPS
Store these brownies in an airtight tin for a day before eating – they improve with keeping.

1 Preheat the oven to 350°F. Line an 8in square pan.

2 Blend the cocoa powder and sugar with the skim milk. Add the bananas, light brown sugar and vanilla extract.

3 Lightly beat the egg whites with a fork. Add the chocolate mixture and continue to beat well. Sift the flour over the mixture and fold in with the oat bran. Pour into the prepared pan.

4 Bake for 40 minutes or until firm. Cool in the pan for 10 minutes, then turn out on a wire rack. Cut into squares and lightly dust with confectioners' sugar before serving.

PEACH JELLY ROLL

A feather-light cake enclosing peach jam – great at snack time.

INGREDIENTS

Serves 6–8
3 eggs
½ cup superfine sugar
¾ cup all-purpose flour, sifted
1 tbsp boiling water
6 tbsp peach jam
confectioners' sugar, for dusting
(optional)

NUTRITION NOTES

Per portion:

Energy	230Kcals/968kJ
Fat	2.45g
Saturated fat	0.67g
Cholesterol	82.50mg
Fiber	0.33g

COOK'S TIP
To decorate the jelly roll, put 4oz glacé icing in a pastry bag fitted with a small writing nozzle and pipe lines over the top.

1 Preheat the oven to 400°F. Grease a 12 x 8 in jelly roll pan and line with nonstick parchment paper. Combine the eggs and sugar in a bowl. Beat with a hand-held electric whisk until thick and mousse-like. (When the whisk is lifted, a trail should remain on the surface of the mixture for at least 15 seconds.)

2 Carefully fold in the flour with a large rubber spatula, then add the boiling water in the same way.

3 Spoon into the prepared pan, spread evenly to the edges and bake for 10–12 minutes, until the cake springs back when lightly pressed.

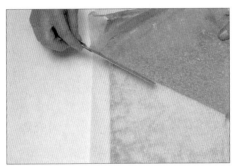

4 Spread a sheet of wax paper on a flat surface, sprinkle it with superfine sugar, then invert the cake on top. Peel off the lining paper.

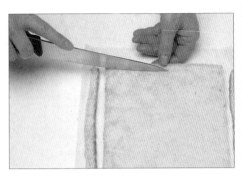

5 Neatly trim the edges of the cake. Make a neat cut two-thirds of the way through the cake, about ½in from the short edge nearest you.

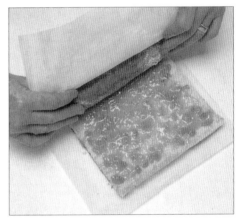

6 Spread the cake with the peach jam and roll up quickly from the partially cut end. Hold in position for a minute, making sure the seam is underneath. Cool on a wire rack. Decorate with glacé icing (see Cook's Tip) or dust with confectioners' sugar before serving.

LEMON CHIFFON CAKE

Lemon mousse provides a tangy filling for this light lemon sponge.

INGREDIENTS

Serves 8
2 eggs
6 tbsp superfine sugar
grated rind of 1 lemon
½ cup sifted all-purpose flour
lemon zest, to decorate

For the filling
2 eggs, separated
6 tbsp sugar
grated rind and juice of 1 lemon
2 tbsp water
1 tbsp gelatin
½ cup low fat cream cheese

For the icing
1 tbsp lemon juice
scant 1 cup confectioners' sugar, sifted

1 Preheat the oven to 350°F. Grease and line an 8in springform cake pan. Whisk the eggs, sugar and lemon rind together with a hand-held electric whisk until thick and mousse-like. Gently fold in the flour, then pour the mixture into the prepared pan.

2 Bake for 20–25 minutes, until the cake springs back when lightly pressed in the center. Turn out on a wire rack to cool. Once cool, split the cake in half horizontally and return the lower half to the clean cake pan.

3 Make the filling. Put the egg yolks, sugar, lemon rind and juice in a bowl. Beat with a hand-held electric whisk until thick, pale and creamy.

4 Pour the water into a heatproof bowl and sprinkle the gelatin on top. Leave until spongy, then stir over simmering water until dissolved. Cool, then whisk into the yolk mixture. Fold in the cream cheese. When the mixture begins to set, whisk the egg whites to soft peaks. Fold the egg whites into the mousse mixture.

5 Pour the lemon mousse over the sponge in the cake pan, spreading it to the edges. Set the second layer of sponge on top and chill until set.

6 Slide a spatula dipped in hot water between the pan and the cake to loosen it, then carefully transfer the cake to a serving plate. Make the icing by adding enough lemon juice to the confectioners' sugar to make a mixture thick enough to coat the back of a wooden spoon. Pour over the cake and spread evenly to the edges. Decorate with the lemon zest.

NUTRITION NOTES	
Per portion:	
Energy	202Kcals/849kJ
Fat	2.81g
Saturated fat	0.79g
Cholesterol	96.41mg
Fiber	0.20g

COOK'S TIP
The mousse should be just setting when the egg whites are added. Speed up this process by placing the bowl of mousse in ice water.

BANANA AND GINGERBREAD SLICES

Very quick to make and
deliciously moist due to the
addition of bananas.

INGREDIENTS

Makes 20
2 cups all-purpose flour
4 tsp ground ginger
2 tsp pumpkin pie spice
1 tsp baking soda
½ cup light brown sugar
4 tbsp sunflower oil
2 tbsp molasses
2 tbsp malt extract
2 eggs
4 tbsp orange juice
3 bananas
⅔ cup raisins

NUTRITION NOTES

Per portion:
Energy	148Kcals/621kJ
Fat	3.07g
Saturated fat	0.53g
Cholesterol	19.30mg
Fiber	0.79g

VARIATION
To make Spiced Honey and
Banana Cake: omit the ground
ginger and add another 1 tsp
mixed spice; omit the malt extract
and the molasses or treacle and
add 4 tbsp strong-flavoured clear
honey instead; and replace the
raisins with either sultanas, or
coarsely chopped dried apricots,
or semi-dried pineapple. If you
choose to use the pineapple, then
you could also replace the orange
juice with fresh pineapple juice.

1 Preheat the oven to 350°F. Lightly
grease and line a 7 x 11 in baking
pan.

2 Sift the flour into a bowl with the
spices and baking soda. Mix in the
sugar with some of the flour and sift it
all into the bowl.

3 Make a well in the center, add the
oil, molasses, malt extract, eggs
and orange juice and mix together
thoroughly.

4 Mash the bananas, add them to
the bowl with the raisins and stir
well to combine.

5 Pour the mixture into the prepared
pan and bake for 35–40 minutes,
until the center springs back when
lightly pressed.

6 Leave the cake in the pan to cool
for 5 minutes, then turn out on a
wire rack and allow to cool completely.
Cut into 20 slices.

COOK'S TIP
If you can't find malt extract, you
can substitute maple extract, but
the flavor is different.

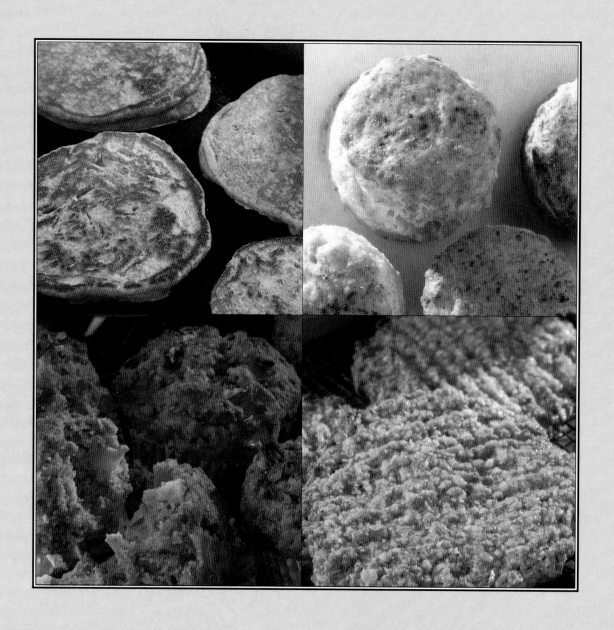

SCONES, MUFFINS, BUNS AND COOKIES

Many scones, muffins, buns and cookies are low in fat and make ideal snacks or treats at any time of day. Try serving them on their own or with a little low fat spread, honey or jam. They are delicious served warm for breakfast or brunch, cold for afternoon tea or packed up and taken out, to enjoy at your leisure. We include a selection of tempting scones, muffins, buns and biscuits, including Pineapple and Cinnamon Drop Scones, Date and Apple Muffins, Banana and Apricot Chelsea Buns, and Oat Crisps.

PINEAPPLE AND CINNAMON DROP SCONES

Making the batter with pineapple juice instead of milk cuts down on fat and adds to the taste.

INGREDIENTS

Makes 24

1 cup self-rising whole-wheat flour
1 cup self-rising white flour
1 tsp ground cinnamon
1 tbsp sugar
1 egg
1¼ cups pineapple juice
½ cup dried pineapple, chopped

NUTRITION NOTES

Per portion:

Energy	15Kcals/215kJ
Fat	0.81g
Saturated fat	0.14g
Cholesterol	8.02mg
Fiber	0.76g

1 Preheat a griddle, heavy frying pan or an electric frying pan. Put the whole-wheat flour in a mixing bowl. Sift in the white flour, add the cinnamon and sugar and make a well in the center.

> **COOK'S TIP**
> Drop scones do not keep well and are best eaten freshly cooked. Other dried fruit, such as apricots or pears, can be used in place of the pineapple.

2 Add the egg with half the pineapple juice and gradually incorporate the surrounding flour to make a smooth batter. Beat in the remaining juice with the chopped pineapple.

3 Lightly grease the griddle or pan. Drop tablespoons of the batter onto the surface, leaving them until they bubble and the bubbles begin to burst.

4 Turn the drop scones with a spatula and cook until the underside is golden brown. Keep the cooked scones warm and moist by wrapping them in a clean napkin while continuing to cook successive batches.

DROP SCONES

These little scones are delicious spread with jam.

── INGREDIENTS ──

Makes 18
2 cups self-rising flour
½ tsp salt
1 tbsp sugar
1 egg, beaten
1¼ cups skim milk
oil, for frying

1 Preheat a griddle, heavy frying pan or an electric frying pan. Sift the flour and salt into a mixing bowl. Stir in the sugar and make a well in the center.

2 Add the egg and half the milk, then gradually incorporate the surrounding flour to make a smooth batter. Beat in the remaining milk.

3 Lightly oil the griddle or pan. Drop tablespoons of the batter onto the surface, leaving them until they bubble and the bubbles begin to burst.

4 Turn the drop scones over with a spatula and cook until the underside is golden brown. Keep the cooked drop scones warm and moist by wrapping them in a clean napkin while cooking successive batches.

── NUTRITION NOTES ──

Per portion:

Energy	64Kcals/270kJ
Fat	1.09g
Saturated fat	0.2g
Cholesterol	11.03mg
Fiber	0.43g

COOK'S TIP
For savory scones, add 2 chopped scallions and 1 tbsp freshly grated Parmesan cheese. Serve with cottage cheese.

CHIVE AND POTATO SCONES

These little scones should be fairly thin, soft and crisp on the outside. They're extremely quick to make, so serve them for breakfast or lunch.

INGREDIENTS

Makes 20
1 lb potatoes
1 cup all-purpose flour, sifted
2 tbsp olive oil
2 tbsp chopped chives
salt and black pepper
low fat margarine (optional)

NUTRITION NOTES

Per portion:
Energy	50Kcals/211kJ
Fat	1.24g
Saturated fat	0.17g
Cholesterol	0
Fiber	0.54g

1 Cook the potatoes in a saucepan of boiling salted water for 20 minutes, then drain thoroughly. Return the potatoes to the clean pan and mash them. Preheat a griddle or heavy frying pan over low heat.

COOK'S TIP
Cook the scones over low heat so that the outsides do not burn before the insides are cooked through.

2 Add the flour, olive oil and chopped chives with a little salt and pepper to the hot mashed potato in the pan. Mix to a soft dough.

3 Roll out the dough on a well-floured surface to a thickness of ¼in and cut out rounds with a 2in plain pastry cutter.

4 Cook the scones in batches on the hot griddle for about 10 minutes, until they are golden brown on both sides. Keep the heat low. Top with a little low fat margarine, if desired, and serve immediately.

CHEESE AND CHIVE SCONES

Makes 9

1 cup self-rising flour
1 cup self-rising whole-wheat flour
¹/₂ tsp salt
3oz feta cheese
1 tbsp chopped fresh chives
²/₃ cup skim milk,
   plus extra for glazing
¹/₄ tsp cayenne pepper

1 Preheat the oven to 400°F. Sift the flours and salt into a mixing bowl, adding any bran left over from the flour in the sifter.

2 Crumble the feta cheese and rub into the dry ingredients. Stir in the chives, then add the milk and mix to a soft dough.

NUTRITION NOTES

Per portion:
Energy	121Kcals/507kJ
Fat	2.24g
Saturated fat	1.13g
Fiber	1.92g

3 Turn out onto a floured surface and knead lightly until smooth. Roll out to ³/₄in thick and cut out nine scones with a 2¹/₂in biscuit cutter.

4 Transfer the scones to a nonstick baking sheet. Brush with skim milk, then sprinkle with the cayenne pepper. Bake for 15 minutes or until the tops are golden brown.

HAM AND TOMATO SCONES

These make an ideal accompaniment for soup. Choose a strongly flavored ham and chop it fairly finely, so that a little goes a long way. Use whole-wheat flour or a mixture of whole-wheat and white flour for extra flavor, texture and fiber.

INGREDIENTS

Makes 12

2 cups self-rising flour
1 tsp dry mustard
1 tsp paprika, plus extra for
   sprinkling
½ tsp salt
2 tbsp soft margarine
1 tbsp chopped fresh basil
1 cup drained sun-dried
   tomatoes in oil, chopped
2oz cooked ham, chopped
¼ –½ cup skim milk, plus extra
   for brushing

1 Preheat the oven to 400°F. Flour a large baking sheet. Sift the flour, mustard, paprika and salt into a bowl. Rub in the margarine until the mixture resembles breadcrumbs.

NUTRITION NOTES

Per portion:

Energy	113Kcals/474kJ
Fat	4.23g
Saturated fat	0.65g
Cholesterol	2.98mg
Fiber	0.65g

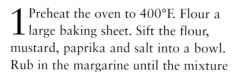

2 Stir in the basil, sun-dried tomatoes and ham, and mix lightly. Pour in enough milk to mix to a soft dough.

3 Turn the dough out onto a lightly floured surface, knead briefly and roll out to a 8 x 6 in rectangle. Cut into 2in squares and arrange on the baking sheet.

4 Brush lightly with milk, sprinkle with paprika and bake for 12–15 minutes. Transfer to a wire rack to cool.

COOK'S TIP
To cut calories and fat, choose dry-packed sun-dried tomatoes and soak them in warm water.

DATE AND APPLE MUFFINS

You will only need one or two of these wholesome muffins per person, because they are very filling.

INGREDIENTS

Makes 12

1¼ *cups self-rising whole-wheat flour*
1¼ *cups self-rising white flour*
1 *tsp ground cinnamon*
1 *tsp baking powder*
2 *tbsp soft margarine*
½ *cup light brown sugar*
1 *apple*
1 *cup apple juice*
2 *tbsp pear and apple spread*
1 *egg, lightly beaten*
½ *cup chopped dates*
1 *tbsp chopped pecans*

1 Preheat the oven to 400°F. Arrange 12 paper cases in a deep muffin tin. Put the whole-wheat flour in a mixing bowl. Sift in the white flour with the cinnamon and baking powder. Rub in the margarine until the mixture resembles bread crumbs, then stir in the brown sugar.

NUTRITION NOTES

Per portion:	
Energy	163Kcals/686kJ
Fat	2.98g
Saturated fat	0.47g
Cholesterol	16.04mg
Fiber	1.97g

2 Quarter and core the apple, chop the flesh finely and set aside. Stir a little of the apple juice with the pear and apple spread until smooth. Mix in the remaining juice, then add to the rubbed-in mixture with the egg. Add the chopped apple to the bowl with the dates. Mix quickly until just combined.

COOK'S TIP
Pear and apple spread is a highly concentrated paste. It is available in health food stores. You can substitute apple butter, but the flavor will not be as intense.

3 Divide the mixture among the muffin cases.

4 Sprinkle with the chopped pecans. Bake the muffins for 20–25 minutes, until golden brown and firm in the middle. Remove to a wire rack and serve while still warm.

RASPBERRY MUFFINS

These muffins are made using baking powder and low fat buttermilk, giving them a light and spongy texture. They are delicious to eat at any time of the day.

NUTRITION NOTES

Per portion:
Energy	171Kcals/719kJ
Fat	4.55g
Saturated fat	0.71g
Cholesterol	16.5mg
Fiber	1.02g

INGREDIENTS

Makes 10–12
2½ cups all-purpose flour
1 tbsp baking powder
½ cup superfine sugar
1 egg
1 cup buttermilk
4 tbsp sunflower oil
5oz raspberries

1 Preheat the oven to 400°F. Arrange 12 paper cases in a deep muffin pan. Sift the flour and baking powder into a mixing bowl, stir in the sugar, then make a well in the center.

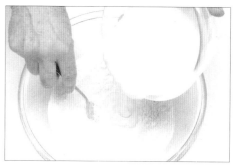

2 Mix the egg, buttermilk and sunflower oil together in a bowl, pour into the flour mixture and mix quickly.

3 Add the raspberries and lightly fold in with a rubber spatula. Spoon the mixture into the paper cases.

4 Bake the muffins for 20–25 minutes, until golden brown and firm in the middle. Transfer to a wire rack and serve warm or cold.

Spiced Banana Muffins

Muffins, with banana for added fiber, make a delicious treat at any time of the day. If desired, slice off the tops and fill with jam.

INGREDIENTS

Makes 12

⅔ cup whole-wheat flour
½ cup all-purpose white flour
2 tsp baking powder
pinch of salt
1 tsp pumpkin pie spice
¼ cup light brown sugar
¼ cup margarine
1 egg, beaten
⅔ cup low-fat milk
grated rind of 1 orange
1 ripe banana
¼ cup rolled oats
scant ¼ cup chopped hazelnuts

1 Preheat the oven to 400°F. Line a muffin pan with 12 large paper cases. Sift together both flours, the baking powder, salt and mixed spice into a bowl, then pour the bran remaining in the sifter into the bowl. Stir in the sugar.

NUTRITION NOTES

Per portion:
Energy	110Kcals/465kJ
Fat	5g
Saturated fat	1g
Cholesterol	17.5mg

2 Melt the margarine and pour it into a mixing bowl. Cool slightly, then beat in the egg, milk and grated orange rind.

3 Gently fold in the dry ingredients. Mash the banana with a fork, then stir it gently into the mixture, being careful not to overmix.

4 Spoon the mixture into the paper cases. Combine the oats and hazelnuts and sprinkle a little of the mixture over each muffin.

5 Bake for 20 minutes until the muffins are well risen and golden, and a skewer inserted in the center comes out clean. Transfer to a wire rack and serve warm or cold.

Banana and Apricot Chelsea Buns

These buns are old favorites given a low fat twist with a delectable fruit filling.

Ingredients

Serves 9
6 tbsp warm skim milk
1 tsp dried yeast
pinch of sugar
2 cups all-purpose flour
2 tsp pumpkin pie spice
½ tsp salt
2 tbsp soft margarine
¼ cup sugar
1 egg

For the filling
1 large ripe banana
1 cup dried apricots
2 tbsp light brown sugar

For the glaze
2 tbsp superfine sugar
2 tbsp water

Cook's Tip
Do not leave the buns in the pans for too long, or the glaze will stick to the sides, making them very difficult to remove.

Nutrition Notes
Per portion:

Energy	214Kcals/901kJ
Fat	3.18g
Saturated fat	0.63g
Cholesterol	21.59mg
Fiber	2.18g

1 Lightly grease an 8-inch square pan. Put the warm milk in a cup and sprinkle the yeast on top. Add a pinch of sugar to help activate the yeast, mix well and let stand for 30 minutes.

2 Sift the flour, spice and salt into a mixing bowl. Stir in the sugar, rub in the margarine, then stir in the yeast mixture and the egg. Gradually mix in the flour to make a soft dough, adding extra milk if needed.

3 Turn out the dough onto a floured surface and knead for 5 minutes until smooth and elastic. Return the dough to the clean bowl, cover with a damp dish towel and let stand in a warm place for about 2 hours, until doubled in bulk.

4 To prepare the filling, mash the banana in a bowl. Using scissors, snip the apricots into pieces, then stir into the banana with the sugar.

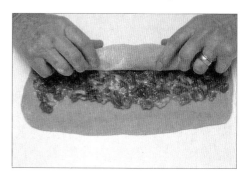

5 Knead the dough on a floured surface for 2 minutes, then roll out to a 12 x 9 in rectangle. Spread the banana and apricot filling over the dough and roll up lengthwise like a jelly roll, with the seam underneath.

6 Cut the roll into 9 buns. Place, cut side down, in the pan, cover and let rise for 30 minutes. Preheat the oven to 400°F and bake for 20–25 minutes. Meanwhile, mix the superfine sugar and water in a small saucepan. Heat, stirring, until dissolved, then boil for 2 minutes. Brush the glaze over the buns while still hot.

OATY CRISPS

These cookies are very crisp and crunchy – ideal to serve with morning coffee.

INGREDIENTS

Makes 18
1¾ cups rolled oats
½ cup light brown sugar
1 egg
4 tbsp sunflower oil
2 tbsp malt extract

NUTRITION NOTES

Per portion:
Energy	86Kcals/360kJ
Fat	3.59g
Saturated fat	0.57g
Cholesterol	10.7mg
Fiber	0.66g

1 Preheat the oven to 375°F. Lightly grease two baking sheets. Mix the rolled oats and sugar in a bowl, breaking up any lumps in the sugar. Add the egg, sunflower oil and malt extract, mix well, then allow to soak for 15 minutes.

2 Using a teaspoon, place small heaps of the mixture well apart on the prepared baking sheets. Press the heaps into 3-inch rounds with the back of a dampened fork.

3 Bake the cookies for 10–15 minutes until golden brown. Let them cool for 1 minute, then remove with a spatula and cool on a wire rack.

COOK'S TIP
Malt extract, a flavoring, isn't widely available; look for it in health-food stores. If you can't find malt extract, you can substitute maple extract, but the flavor is different.

OATCAKES

Try serving these oatcakes with reduced-fat hard cheeses. They are delicious topped with thick honey for breakfast.

INGREDIENTS

Makes 8

1 cup rolled oats, plus extra
*   for sprinkling*
½ tsp salt
pinch of baking soda
1 tbsp butter
5 tbsp water

1 Preheat the oven to 300°F. Mix the oatmeal with the salt and baking soda in a bowl.

2 Melt the butter with the water in a small saucepan. Bring to a boil, then add to the oatmeal mixture and mix to a moist dough.

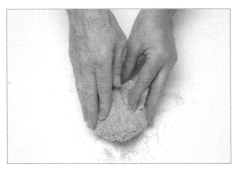

3 Turn the dough onto a surface sprinkled with oatmeal and knead to a smooth ball. Turn a large baking sheet upside-down, grease it, sprinkle it lightly with oatmeal and place the ball of dough on top. Sprinkle the dough with oatmeal, then roll out to a 10-inch round.

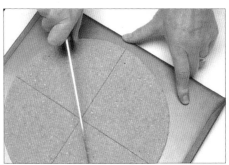

4 Cut the round into eight sections, ease them apart slightly and bake for 50–60 minutes, until crisp. Allow the oatcakes to cool on the baking sheet, then remove with a metal spatula.

COOK'S TIP
To achieve a neat round, place a 10in cake board or plate on top of the oatcake. Cut away any excess dough with a sharp knife.

NUTRITION NOTES

Per portion:

Energy	102Kcals/427kJ
Fat	3.43g
Saturated fat	0.66g
Cholesterol	0.13mg
Fiber	1.49g

BREADS AND QUICK BREADS

Breads and quick breads can be ideal low fat snacks at any time of day. Bread is the perfect accompaniment to many meals, and moist, flavorful quick bread, served with a warm beverage, is a delightful treat. Among the appetizing selection of recipes presented here are Rosemary and Sea Salt Focaccia, Prosciutto and Parmesan Bread, Pear and Raisin Quick Bread and Banana and Cardamom Bread.

ROSEMARY AND SEA SALT FOCACCIA

Focaccia is an Italian flat bread made with olive oil. Here it is given added flavor with rosemary and coarse sea salt.

INGREDIENTS

Serves 8
3 cups all-purpose flour
1/2 tsp salt
2 tsp rapid-rise dried yeast
1 cup lukewarm water
3 tbsp olive oil
1 small red onion
leaves from 1 large rosemary sprig
1 tsp coarse sea salt
oil, for greasing

1 Sift the flour and salt into a large mixing bowl. Stir in the yeast, then make a well in the middle of the dry ingredients. Pour in the water and 2 tablespoons of the oil. Mix well, adding a little more water if the mixture seems too dry.

COOK'S TIP
Use flavored olive oil, such as chili or herb oil, for extra flavor. Whole-wheat flour or a mixture of whole-wheat and white flour works well with this recipe.

2 Turn the dough onto a lightly floured surface and knead for about 10 minutes, until smooth and elastic.

3 Place the dough in a greased bowl, cover and leave in a warm place for about 1 hour, until doubled in size. Punch down and knead the dough for 2–3 minutes.

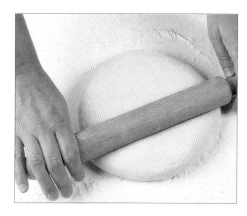

4 Meanwhile, preheat the oven to 425°F. Roll out the dough to a large circle about 1/2in thick, and transfer to a greased baking sheet. Brush with the remaining oil.

5 Halve the onion and slice it into thin wedges. Sprinkle over the dough, with the rosemary and sea salt, pressing lightly.

6 Using a finger, make deep indentations in the dough. Cover the surface with greased plastic wrap, then let rise in a warm place for 30 minutes. Remove the plastic and bake for 25–30 minutes, until golden. Serve warm.

NUTRITION NOTES

Per portion:
Energy	191Kcals/807kJ
Fat	4.72g
Saturated fat	0.68g
Cholesterol	0
Fiber	1.46g

OLIVE AND OREGANO BREAD

This is an excellent accompaniment to all salads and is particularly good served warm.

INGREDIENTS

Serves 8–10
1¼ cups warm water
1 tsp dried yeast
pinch of sugar
1 tbsp olive oil
1 onion, chopped
4 cups all-purpose flour
1 tsp salt
¼ tsp black pepper
⅓ cup pitted black olives,
  coarsely chopped
1 tbsp black olive paste
1 tbsp chopped fresh oregano
1 tbsp chopped fresh parsley

NUTRITION NOTES

Per portion:

Energy	202Kcals/847kJ
Fat	3.28g
Saturated fat	0.46g
Cholesterol	0
Fiber	22.13g

1 Put half the warm water in a cup. Sprinkle the yeast on top. Add the sugar, mix well and allow to stand for 10 minutes.

2 Heat the olive oil in a small frying pan and fry the onion gently until golden brown.

3 Sift the flour into a mixing bowl with the salt and pepper. Make a well in the center. Add the yeast mixture, the fried onion (with the oil), the olives, olive paste, herbs and remaining water. Gradually incorporate the flour and mix to a soft dough, adding a little extra water if necessary.

4 Turn the dough onto a floured surface and knead for 5 minutes, until smooth and elastic. Place in a mixing bowl, cover with a damp dish-towel and leave in a warm place to rise for about 2 hours, until the dough has doubled in bulk. Lightly grease a baking sheet.

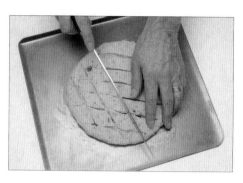

5 Turn the dough onto a floured surface and knead again for a few minutes. Shape into an 8in round and place on the prepared baking sheet. Using a large sharp knife, make crisscross cuts over the top. Cover and let stand in a warm place for 30 minutes until well risen. Preheat the oven to 425°F.

6 Dust the loaf with a little flour. Bake for 10 minutes, then lower the oven temperature to 400°F. Bake for 20 more minutes, or until the loaf sounds hollow when tapped underneath. Transfer to a wire rack and allow to cool slightly before serving.

COOK'S TIP
If fresh herbs are not available, use 1–2 tsp dried herbs instead. Omit the olives and olive paste and use chopped sun-dried tomatoes and sun-dried tomato paste, for a tasty change.

RYE BREAD

Rye bread is popular in northern Europe and makes an excellent base for open sandwiches – add a low fat topping of your choice.

INGREDIENTS

Serves 16
3 cups whole-wheat flour
2 cups rye flour
1 cup all-purpose flour
1½ tsp salt
2 tbsp caraway seeds
2 cups warm water
2 tsp dried yeast
pinch of sugar
2 tbsp molasses

1 Put the flours and salt in a bowl. Set aside 1 tsp of the caraway seeds and add the rest to the bowl.

2 Put half the water in a cup. Sprinkle the yeast on top. Add the sugar, mix well and let stand for 10 minutes.

3 Make a well in the flour mixture, then add the yeast mixture with the molasses and the remaining water. Gradually incorporate the flour and mix to a soft dough, adding a little water if necessary.

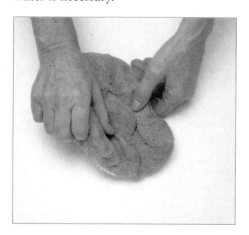

4 Turn the dough onto a floured surface and knead for 5 minutes, until smooth and elastic. Return to the clean bowl, cover with a damp dish-towel and leave in a warm place for about 2 hours, until doubled in bulk. Grease a baking sheet.

NUTRITION NOTES

Per portion:

Energy	156Kcals/655kJ
Fat	1.2g
Saturated fat	0.05g
Cholesterol	0
Fiber	4.53g

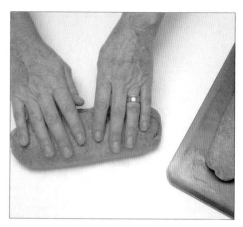

5 Turn the dough onto a floured surface and knead for 2 minutes. Divide the dough in half, then shape into two 9in long oval loaves. Flatten the loaves slightly and place them on a baking sheet.

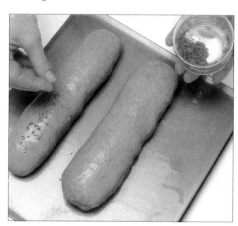

6 Brush the loaves with water and sprinkle with the remaining caraway seeds. Cover and let stand in a warm place for about 40 minutes, until well risen. Preheat the oven to 400°F. Bake the loaves for 30 minutes or until they sound hollow when tapped underneath. Cool on a wire rack. Serve the bread plain, or slice and add a low fat topping.

SODA BREAD

Finding the bread box empty need never be a problem again when your repertoire includes a recipe for soda bread. It takes only a few minutes to make and needs no rising or proving. If possible, eat soda bread while still warm from the oven as it does not keep well.

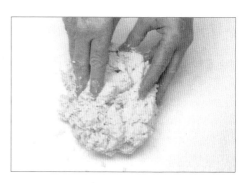

INGREDIENTS

Serves 8
4 cups all-purpose flour
1 tsp salt
1 tsp baking soda
1 tsp cream of tartar
1½ cups buttermilk

1 Preheat the oven to 425°F. Flour a baking sheet. Sift all the dry ingredients into a mixing bowl and make a small well in the center.

2 Add the buttermilk and mix quickly to a soft dough. Turn onto a floured surface and knead lightly. Shape into a round about 7in across and put on the baking sheet.

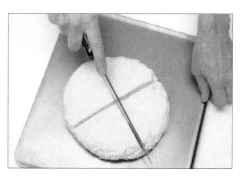

3 Cut a deep cross on top of the loaf and sprinkle with a little flour. Bake for 25–30 minutes, then transfer the soda bread to a wire rack to cool.

COOK'S TIP
Soda bread needs a light hand. The ingredients should be mixed together quickly in the bowl and kneaded very briefly. The aim is to get rid of the largest cracks, as the dough will become tough if it is handled for too long.

NUTRITION NOTES

Per portion:	
Energy	230Kcals/967kJ
Fat	1.03g
Saturated fat	0.24g
Cholesterol	0.88mg
Fiber	1.94g

PEAR AND RAISIN QUICK BREAD

This is an ideal quick bread to make when pears are plentiful – an excellent use for windfalls.

INGREDIENTS

Serves 6–8
¼ cup rolled oats
¼ cup light brown sugar
2 tbsp pear or apple juice
2 tbsp sunflower oil
1 large or 2 small pears
1 cup self-rising flour
¾ cup raisins
½ tsp baking powder
2 tsp pumpkin pie spice
1 egg

1 Preheat the oven to 350°F. Grease and line a 1 lb loaf tin with non-stick parchment paper. Put the oats in a bowl with the sugar, pour over the pear or apple juice and oil, mix well and allow to stand for 15 minutes.

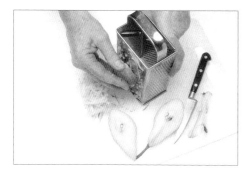

2 Quarter, core and coarsely grate the pear(s). Add to the oat mixture with the flour, raisins, baking powder, pumpkin pie spice and egg, then combine thoroughly.

3 Spoon the mixture into the prepared loaf pan and level the top. Bake for 50–60 minutes or until a skewer inserted into the center comes out clean.

COOK'S TIP
Health food shops sell concentrated pear and apple juice, ready for diluting as needed.

4 Transfer the quick bread onto a wire rack and peel off the lining paper. Allow to cool completely.

NUTRITION NOTES

Per portion:
Energy	200Kcals/814kJ
Fat	4.61g
Saturated fat	0.79g
Cholesterol	27.50mg
Fiber	1.39g

PROSCIUTTO AND PARMESAN BREAD

This nourishing bread is almost a meal in itself.

INGREDIENTS

Serves 8
2 cups self-rising whole-wheat flour
2 cups self-rising white flour
1 tsp baking powder
1 tsp salt
1 tsp black pepper
3oz prosciutto
2 tbsp freshly grated Parmesan cheese
2 tbsp chopped fresh parsley
3 tbsp whole-grain mustard
1½ cups buttermilk
skim milk, to glaze

1 Preheat the oven to 400°F. Flour a baking sheet. Place the whole-wheat flour in a bowl and sift in the white flour, baking powder and salt. Add the pepper and the ham. Set aside about 1 tbsp of the grated Parmesan and stir the rest into the flour mixture with the parsley. Make a well in the center.

2 Mix the mustard and buttermilk, pour into the flour and quickly mix to a soft dough.

3 Turn the dough onto a floured surface and knead briefly. Shape into an oval loaf, brush with milk and sprinkle with the Parmesan cheese. Put the loaf on the prepared baking sheet.

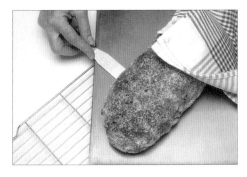

4 Bake the loaf for 25–30 minutes. Allow to cool before serving.

CARAWAY BREAD STICKS

Ideal to nibble with drinks, these can be made with all sorts of other seeds – try cumin seeds, poppy seeds or celery seeds.

INGREDIENTS

Makes about 20
²⁄₃ *cup warm water*
½ *tsp dried yeast*
pinch of sugar
2 cups all-purpose flour
½ *tsp salt*
2 tsp caraway seeds

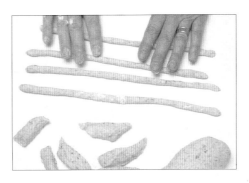

3 Preheat the oven to 425°F. Turn the dough onto a lightly floured surface and knead for 5 minutes, until smooth. Divide the mixture into 20 pieces and roll each into a 12in stick.

4 Arrange the sticks on the baking sheets, leaving room to allow for rising.

5 Bake the bread sticks for 10–12 minutes, until golden brown. Cool on the baking sheets.

NUTRITION NOTES	
Per portion:	
Energy	45Kcals/189kJ
Fat	0.24g
Saturated fat	0.02g
Cholesterol	0
Fiber	0.3g

1 Grease two baking sheets. Put the warm water in a cup. Sprinkle the yeast on top. Add the sugar, mix well and let stand for 10 minutes.

2 Sift the flour and salt into a mixing bowl, stir in the caraway seeds and make a well in the center. Add the yeast mixture and gradually incorporate the flour to make a soft dough, adding a little water if necessary.

CHEESE AND ONION HERB STICKS

An extremely tasty bread that is very good with soups or salads. Use an extra-strong cheese to give plenty of flavor without piling on the fat.

INGREDIENTS

Makes 2 sticks, each serving 4–6
1¼ cups warm water
1 tsp dried yeast
pinch of sugar
1 tbsp sunflower oil
1 red onion, finely chopped
4 cups all-purpose flour
1 tsp salt
1 tsp dry mustard
3 tbsp chopped fresh herbs,
    such as thyme, parsley, marjoram
    or sage
¾ cup grated reduced fat cheddar
cheese

NUTRITION NOTES

Per portion:
Energy	210Kcals/882kJ
Fat	3.16g
Saturated fat	0.25g
Cholesterol	3.22mg
Fiber	1.79g

COOK'S TIP
To make Onion and Coriander Sticks, omit the cheese, herbs and mustard. Add 1 tbsp ground coriander and 3 tbsp chopped cilantro instead.

1 Put the water in a cup. Sprinkle the yeast on top. Add the sugar, mix well and let stand for 10 minutes.

2 Heat the oil in a small frying pan and fry the onion until it is well colored.

3 Stir the flour, salt and mustard into a mixing bowl, then add the herbs. Set aside 2 tbsp of the cheese. Stir the rest into the flour mixture and make a well in the center. Add the yeast mixture with the fried onions and oil, then gradually incorporate the flour and mix to a soft dough, adding extra water if necessary.

4 Turn the dough onto a floured surface and knead for 5 minutes, until smooth and elastic. Return to the clean bowl, cover with a damp dish-towel and let sit in a warm place to rise for about 2 hours, until doubled in bulk. Lightly grease two baking sheets.

5 Turn the dough onto a floured surface, knead briefly, then divide the mixture in half and roll each piece into a 12in long stick. Place each stick on a baking sheet and make diago cuts along the top.

6 Sprinkle the sticks with the reserved cheese. Cover and let stand for 30 minutes until well risen. Preheat the oven to 425°F. Bake the sticks for 25 minutes or until they sound hollow when tapped underneath.

WHOLE-WHEAT ROLLS

These make excellent picnic fare, filled with cottage cheese, tuna, salad and low fat mayonnaise. They are also very good served warm with soup.

INGREDIENTS

Makes 8
1¼ cups warm water
1 tsp dried yeast
pinch of sugar
4 cups malted brown flour
1 tsp salt
1 tbsp malt extract
1 tbsp rolled oats

NUTRITION NOTES

Per portion:

Energy	223Kcals/939kJ
Fat	1.14g
Saturated fat	0.16g
Cholesterol	0
Fiber	3.10g

COOK'S TIP
To make a large loaf, shape the dough into a round, flatten it slightly and bake for 30–40 minutes. Test by tapping the base of the loaf – if it sounds hollow, it is cooked.

1 Put half the warm water in a cup. Sprinkle in the yeast. Add the sugar, mix well and let stand for 10 minutes.

2 Put the malted brown flour and salt in a mixing bowl and make a well in the center. Add the yeast mixture with the malt extract and the remaining water. Gradually incorporate the flour and mix to a soft dough.

3 Turn the dough onto a floured surface and knead for 5 minutes, until smooth and elastic. Return to a clean bowl, cover with a damp towel and put in a warm place to rise for about 2 hours, until doubled in bulk.

4 Lightly grease a large baking sheet. Turn the dough onto a floured surface, knead for 2 minutes, then divide into eight pieces. Shape the pieces into balls and flatten them with the palm of your hand to make neat 4in rounds.

5 Place the rounds on the prepared baking sheet, cover loosely with a large plastic bag (ballooning it to trap the air inside), and let stand in a warm place until the rolls are well risen. Preheat the oven to 425°F.

6 Brush the rolls with water, sprinkle with the oats and bake for about 20–25 minutes or until they sound hollow when tapped underneath. Cool on a wire rack, then serve with the low fat filling of your choice.

POPPY SEED ROLLS

Pile these soft rolls in a basket and serve them for breakfast or with dinner.

INGREDIENTS

Makes 12
1¼ cups warm skim milk
1 tsp dried yeast
pinch of sugar
4 cups all-purpose flour
1 tsp salt
1 egg, lightly beaten

For the topping
1 egg, beaten
poppy seeds

NUTRITION NOTES

Per portion:
Energy	160Kcals/674kJ
Fat	2.42g
Saturated fat	0.46g
Cholesterol	32.58mg
Fiber	1.16g

1 Put half the warm milk in a small bowl. Sprinkle the yeast on top. Add the sugar, mix well and let stand for 30 minutes.

2 Sift the flour and salt into a mixing bowl. Make a well in the center and pour in the yeast mixture and the egg. Gradually incorporate the flour, adding enough of the remaining milk to mix to a soft dough.

3 Turn the dough onto a floured surface and knead for 5 minutes, until smooth and elastic. Return to the clean bowl, cover with a damp dish-towel and put in a warm place to rise for about 1 hour, until doubled in bulk.

4 Lightly grease two baking sheets. Turn the dough onto a floured surface. Knead for 2 minutes, then cut into 12 pieces and shape into rolls.

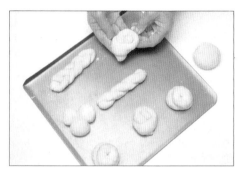

5 Place the rolls on the prepared baking sheets, cover loosely with a large plastic bag (ballooning it to trap the air inside) and allow to stand in a warm place until the rolls have doubled in bulk. Preheat the oven to 425°F.

6 Glaze the rolls with beaten egg, sprinkle with poppy seeds and bake for 12–15 minutes, until golden brown. Transfer to a wire rack to cool.

COOK'S TIP
Use rapid-rise dried yeast if you prefer. Add it directly to the dry ingredients and mix with hand-hot milk. The rolls will only require one rising (see package instructions). Vary the toppings. Linseed, sesame seeds and caraway seeds are all good; try adding caraway seeds to the dough, too, for extra flavor.

BANANA AND CARDAMOM BREAD

The combination of banana and cardamom is delicious in this soft-textured moist loaf. It is perfect for snacks, served with low fat spread and jam. No fat is used or needed to make this delicious loaf, creating a healthy low fat bread for all to enjoy.

INGREDIENTS

Serves 6
²/₃ *cup warm water*
1 tsp dried yeast
pinch of sugar
10 cardamom pods
3¹/₂ cups all-purpose flour
1 tsp salt
2 tbsp malt extract
2 ripe bananas, mashed
1 tsp sesame seeds

1 Put the warm water in a small bowl. Sprinkle the yeast on top. Add the sugar, mix well and let stand for 10 minutes.

2 Split the cardamom pods. Remove the seeds and chop them finely.

3 Sift the flour and salt into a mixing bowl and make a well in the center. Add the yeast mixture with the malt extract, chopped cardamom seeds and bananas.

4 Gradually incorporate the flour and mix to a soft dough, adding a little extra water if necessary. Turn the dough onto a floured surface and knead for about 5 minutes, until smooth and elastic. Return to the clean bowl, cover with a damp dishtowel and allow to rise for about 2 hours until doubled in bulk.

NUTRITION NOTES

Per portion:
Energy	299Kcals/1254kJ
Fat	1.55g
Saturated fat	0.23g
Cholesterol	0
Fiber	2.65g

5 Grease a baking sheet. Turn the dough onto a floured surface, knead briefly, then divide into three and shape into a braid. Place the braid on the baking sheet and cover loosely with a plastic bag (ballooning it to trap the air). Let stand until well risen. Preheat the oven to 425°F.

6 Brush the plait lightly with water and sprinkle with the sesame seeds. Bake for 10 minutes, then lower the oven temperature to 400°F. Cook for 15 more minutes, or until the loaf sounds hollow when it is tapped underneath. Cool on a wire rack.

COOK'S TIP
Make sure the bananas are really ripe, so that they impart maximum flavor to the bread. If you prefer, place the dough in one piece in a 1 lb loaf pan and bake for an extra 5 minutes. As well as being low in fat, bananas are a good source of potassium, therefore making an ideal nutritious, low fat snack.

Swedish Golden Raisin Bread

A lightly sweetened fruit bread that is delicious served warm. It is also excellent toasted and topped with low fat spread.

Ingredients

Serves 8–10

⅔ *cup warm water*
1 tsp dried yeast
1 tbsp honey
2 cups whole-wheat flour
2 cups all-purpose flour
1 tsp salt
⅔ *cup golden raisins*
½ *cup walnuts, finely chopped*
¾ *cup warm skim milk,*
  plus extra for glazing

Nutrition Notes

Per portion:

Energy	273Kcals/1145kJ
Fat	4.86g
Saturated fat	0.57g
Cholesterol	0.39mg
Fiber	3.83g

1 Put the water in a small bowl. Sprinkle the yeast on top. Add a few drops of the honey to help activate the yeast, mix well and allow to stand for 10 minutes.

2 Put the flours in a mixing bowl with the salt and raisins. Set aside 1 tablespoon of the walnuts and add the rest to the bowl. Mix together lightly and make a well in the center.

3 Add the yeast mixture to the flour mixture with the milk and remaining honey. Gradually incorporate the flour, mixing to a soft dough; add a little extra water if you need to.

4 Turn the dough onto a floured surface and knead for 5 minutes, until smooth and elastic. Return to the clean bowl, cover with a damp dish-towel and put in a warm place to rise for about 2 hours, until doubled in bulk. Grease a baking sheet.

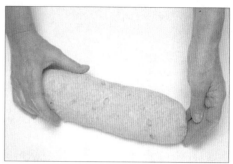

5 Turn the dough onto a floured surface and form into a 11in long sausage shape. Place on the baking sheet. Make some diagonal cuts down the whole length of the loaf.

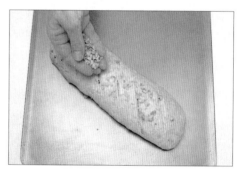

6 Brush the loaf with milk to glaze, sprinkle with the reserved walnuts and set aside to rise for about 40 minutes. Preheat the oven to 425°F. Bake the loaf for 10 minutes. Lower the oven temperature to 400°F and bake for about 20 more minutes, or until the loaf sounds hollow when tapped underneath.

Cook's Tip
To make Apple and Hazelnut Bread, replace the raisins with two chopped eating apples and use chopped toasted hazelnuts instead of the walnuts. Add 1 tsp ground cinnamon with the flour.

Index